HOW FEDERAL LAWS ARE MADE

 **WANT Publishing Company**
1511 K Street, N.W.
Washington, DC 20005

Printed by Catterton Printing Co.,
Washington, D.C.
United States of America

ISBN: 0-942008-01-4

Library of Congress Catalog Card Number: 81-70748

HOW FEDERAL LAWS ARE MADE

— TABLE OF CONTENTS —

— TABLE OF CONTENTS (Continued) —

INTRODUCTION

HOW FEDERAL LAWS ARE MADE has a three-fold purpose:

— To provide an easily-readable outline of the steps in the Federal lawmaking process, from the origin of an idea for a legislative proposal, to its publication as a statute, to the issuance of agency rules and regulations.

— To serve as a handy guide to the use of the published reports of United States laws and regulations, including the Slip Law, the U.S. Statutes at Large, the U.S. Code, and the Federal Register System. The *Congressional Record* is also discussed.

— To provide a basic explanation of the budget process, for both Congress and the Executive Branch.

Federal lawmaking impacts us all. While legislation has grown dramatically in volume and complexity in recent years, so has the opportunity for public participation in governmental decisions, the opportunity for all sides to be heard and make their voices known. The objective of *HOW FEDERAL LAWS ARE MADE* is to enable the reader to gain a better understanding of the Federal lawmaking process and the vital role it plays in our society, and in so doing encourage participation in that process.

HOW FEDERAL LAWS ARE MADE is intended as a nontechnical reading and reference source. Guides to further reading are given when appropriate. The publication is divided into four major parts.

• Part I (beginning on page 2) discusses how the Congress considers and passes legislation. Emphasis is given as to how Congressional committees function in this process. Because the large majority of laws originate in the House of Representatives, this discussion will be directed principally to procedures of that body.

• Part II (beginning on page 48) provides a basic explanation of the budget process, for both Congress and the Executive Branch. A glossary of terms is included.

• Part III (beginning on page 75) explains — in a carefully illustrated step-by-step process — how to find U.S. Statutes and U.S. Code Citations.

• Part IV (beginning on page 86) is a guide to the use of the *Federal Register* and the *Code of Federal Regulations*.

Our discussion in Part I below will begin with a capsule summary of the legislative process, and proceed to a step-by-step explanation of how a bill is enacted into law.

PART I
THE LEGISLATIVE PROCESS

CAPSULE SUMMARY

In a nutshell, this is the general procedure through which legislation is enacted into law: A member of Congress introduces a bill. It is referred to a committee and in turn to a subcommittee. The subcommittee holds hearings on the bill and then amends and sends it back to the full committee. The full committee may amend the bill further and then issue a report on it. The bill is now ready for floor action where it may be debated and further amended. If it passes, it is then sent to the other chamber where the same process is reenacted.

Frequently, each chamber is working simultaneously on the same or similar legislation. Once both chambers have passed their versions of a bill, they can reconcile any differences by agreeing to or modifying the amendments of the other chamber — or by sending the measure to a conference committee. (See chart on following page.)

The conference committee tries to arrive at language acceptable to both bodies. Once both Senate and House agree on the exact language, the legislation is sent to the President for his approval and signature into law. Should the President veto it, the Congress would normally have the option of trying to override his veto. But it's not always this straight-forward and the discussion to follow attempts to show what intricacies may be involved.

The chart on the next page shows the typical path of two pieces of similar legislation as they work their way through the Senate and House of Representatives, respectively.

THE CONGRESS

Article I, section 1, of the United States Constitution, provides that—

All legislative Powers herein granted shall be vested in a Congress of the United States, which shall consist of a Senate and House of Representatives.

The Senate is composed of 100 Members — two from each state, irrespective of population or area. A Senator must be at least 30 years of age, and have been a citizen of the United States for nine years and, when elected, a resident of the State from which he is chosen. The term of office is six years and one-third of the total membership is elected every second year. The terms of both Senators from a particular State are so arranged that they do not terminate at the same time. Of the two Senators from a State serving at the same time, the one who was elected first — or if both were elected at the same time, the one elected for a full term — is referred to as the "senior" Senator from that State. The other is referred to as the "junior" Senator. Each Senator has one vote.

The House of Representatives is composed of 435 Members elected every two years from districts within the 50 States, apportioned as to their total populations. A law enacted in 1967 has abolished all "at-large" elections (i.e., Members elected by the voters of the entire State rather than in a Congressional district within the State) except, of course, in States entitled to only one Representative.

A Representative must be at least 25 years of age and have been a citizen of the United States for seven years and, when elected, a resident of the State in which he is chosen. In case of the death or resignation of a Member during his term, the governor of his State may call a special election for the choosing of a successor to serve for the unexpired portion of that term. Each Representative has one vote.

In addition to the Representatives from 50 States, there is a Resident Commissioner from the Commonwealth of Puerto Rico, and Delegates to the House of Representatives from

TYPICAL PATH OF LEGISLATION

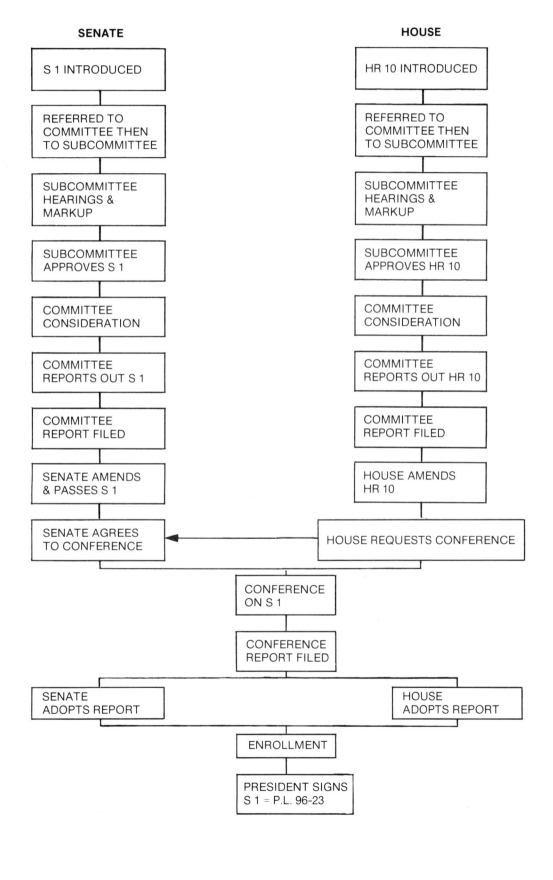

the District of Columbia,[1] Guam, the Virgin Islands, and the American Samoa. The Resident Commissioner and the Delegates have most of the prerogatives of Representatives, with the important exception of the right to vote on matters before the House. But they can vote in committee session.

A Congress lasts for two years and is divided into two annual sessions. Unlike some other parliamentary bodies, both the Senate and the House of Representatives have equal legislative functions and powers (except that only the House of Representatives have equal legislative functions and powers (except that only the House of Representatives may initiate revenue bills), and the designation of one as the "upper" House and the other as the "lower" House is not appropriate.

The Constitution authorizes each House to determine the rules of its proceedings. Pursuant to that authority the House of Representatives adopts its rules on the opening day of each Congress. The Senate, which considers itself a continuing body, operates under rules that it amends from time to time.

The chief function of the Congress is the making of laws. The Senate has, in addition, the function of advising and consenting to treaties and to certain nominations by the President. In the matter of impeachments, the House of Representatives presents the charges — a function similar to that of grand juries — and the Senate sits as a court to try the impeachment.

Both Houses meet in joint session on January 6th, following a presidential election, to count the electoral votes.[2] If no candidate receives a majority of the total electoral votes, the House of Representatives chooses the President from among the three candidates having the largest number of votes, and the Senate chooses the Vice President from the two candidates having the largest number of votes for that office.

SOURCES OF LEGISLATION

Sources of ideas for legislation are unlimited, and proposed drafts of bills originate in many diverse quarters. Most prominent is the idea and draft conceived by a Member himself. This may emanate from his election campaign during which he had promised, if elected, to introduce legislation on a particular subject. His entire campaign may have been based upon one or more such proposals. Or, through his experience after taking office he may have become aware of the need for the amendment or repeal of existing laws or the enactment of a statute in an entirely new field.

In addition, pressure groups — whether business or social-service orientated — may not only lobby a proposal but also provide the technical assistance for drafting the legislation.

In modern times the "executive communication" has become a prolific source of legislative proposals. This is usually in the form of a letter from a member of the President's Cabinet or the head of an independent agency — or even from the President himself — transmitting a draft of a proposed bill to the Speaker of the House of Representatives and the President of the Senate. Despite the system of separation of powers, the Constitution imposes an obligation on the President to report to the Congress from time to time on the state Union and to recommend for consideration such measures as he considers necessary and expedient.[3] Many of these executive communications follow on the President's message to Congress on the state of the Union. The communication is then referred to the standing committee (see below, p.7) having jurisdiction of the subject matter embraced in the proposal. Since a bill may only be introduced by a Member of Congress, the chairman

---

[1] Under the 1973 D.C. Home Rule Act passed by Congress, the District of Columbia was given self-rule authority similar to that granted most other cities by their respective state governments, with the exception that in the District of Columbia the city is required to send most measures passed by its city council to Congress, where a majority of either the House or Senate could overturn any such measure within 30 congressional working days. In the eight years of "home rule" for the District, Congress has used this veto power on two occasions.

[2] U.S.C.§15. See Part III below on "How to Find U.S. Statutes and U.S. Code Citations.

[3] U.S. Constitution, Art. II, Sec. 3.

of that committee usually introduces the bill promptly either in the form in which it was received or with changes.

This practice prevails even when the majority of the House and the President are not of the same political party, although there is no constitutional or statutory requirement that a bill be introduced to effectuate the President's recommendations.

The most important of the regular executive communications is the annual message from the President transmitting the proposed budget to the Congress. This, together with testimony by officials of the various branches of the Government before the Appropriations Committees of the House and Senate, is the basis of the several appropriation bills that are drafted by the House Committee on Appropriations. (See Part II below for a discussion of the budget process.)

Several of the executive departments and independent agencies have staffs of trained legislative counsels whose functions include the drafting of bills to be forwarded to the Congress with a request for their enactment.

The drafting of statutes is an art that requires considerable skill, knowledge, and experience. In some instances, a draft is the result of a study covering a period of a year or more by a commission or committee designated by the President or one of his Cabinet officers. The Administrative Procedure Act and the Uniform Code of Military Justice are only two of many examples of enactments resulting from such studies. Similarly, Congressional committees sometimes draft bills after studies and hearings covering periods of a year or more. Bills to codify the laws relating to crimes and criminal procedure, the judiciary and judicial procedure, the Armed Forces, and other subjects, have each required several years of preparation.

FORMS OF CONGRESSIONAL ACTION

Once legislation is drafted, it is introduced in Congress in one of four principal forms, including: the bill, the joint resolution, the concurrent resolution, and the simple resolution. By far the most customary form used in both Houses is the bill. During the 96th Congress (1979-1980), there were a total of 11,722 bills introduced, 8,456 in the House and 3,266 in the Senate.

The discussion below will be confined generally to the procedure on a House of Representatives bill, though comments will be made about Senate procedure as well.

BILLS

A bill is the form used for most legislation, whether permanent or temporary, general or special, public or private.

The form of a House bill is as follows:

A BILL

For the establishment, etc. [as the title may be].

Be it enacted by the Senate and House of Representatives of the
United States of America in Congress assembled, That, etc.

Bills may originate in either the House of Representatives or the Senate, with one notable exception. The Constitution provides that all bills for raising revenue shall originate in the House of Representatives,[1] but the Senate may propose or concur with amendments, as on

---

[1]U.S. Constitution, Art. 1, Sec. 7.

other bills. General appropriation bills also originate in the House of Representatives.

A bill originating in the House of Representatives is designated by the letters "H.R." followed by a number that it retains throughout all its parliamentary stages. The letters signify "House of Representatives" and not, as it sometimes supposed, "House resolution". A Senate bill is designated by the letter "S." followed by its number. (See series of figures below, beginning on page 34).

A bill that has been agreed to in identical form by both bodies becomes the law of the land only after—

    (1) Presidential approval;
    (2) failure by the President to return it with his objections to the House in which it originated within 10 days while the Congress is in session;
    (3) the overriding of a Presidential veto by a two-thirds vote in each House.

It does not become law without the President's signature if the Congress by their adjournment prevent its return with his objections. This is known as a "pocket veto".

JOINT RESOLUTIONS

Joint resolutions may originate either in the House of Representatives or in the Senate — not, as may be supposed, jointly in both Houses. There is little practical difference between a bill and a joint resolution and, although the latter are not as numerous as bills, the two forms are often used indiscriminately. Statutes that have been initiated as bills have later been amended by a joint resolution, and vice versa. Both are subject to the same procedure — with the exception of a joint resolution proposing an amendment to the Constitution. Such a resolution, on approval by two-thirds of both Houses, is sent directly to the Administrator of General Services for submission to the several States for ratification. It is not presented to the President for his approval.

The form of a House joint resolution is as follows:

JOINT RESOLUTION

Authorizing, etc. [as the title may be].

Resolved by the Senate and House of Representatives of the United
States of America in Congress assembled, That all, etc.

The resolving clause is identical in both House and Senate joint resolutions. It is frequently preceded by one or more "whereas" clauses indicating the necessity for or the desirability of the joint resolution.

The term "joint" does not signify simultaneous introduction and consideration in both Houses.

A joint resolution originating in the House of Representatives is designated "H.J. Res." followed by its individual number which it retains throughout all its parliamentary stages. One originating in the Senate is designated "S.J. Res." followed by its number.

Joint resolutions become law in the same manner as bills.

CONCURRENT RESOLUTIONS

Matters affecting the operations of both Houses are usually initiated by means of concurrent resolutions. These are not normally legislative in character but used merely for expressing certain principles, opinions, and purposes of the two Houses. They are not equivalent to a bill and their use is narrowly limited.

The term "concurrent" does not signify simultaneous introduction and consideration in both Houses.

A concurrent resolution originating in the House of Representatives is designated "H. Con. Res." followed by its individual number, while a Senate concurrent resolution is designated "S. Con. Res." together with its number. On approval by both Houses, they are signed by the Clerk of the House and the Secretary of the Senate and transmitted to the Administrator of General Services for publication in a special part of the Statutes at Large. (See Part III below for full explanation of the "Publication" process.) They are not presented to the President for action as are bills and joint resolutions.

SIMPLE RESOLUTIONS

A matter concerning the operation of either House alone is initiated by a simple resolution. A resolution affecting the House of Representatives is designated "H. Res." followed by its number, while a Senate resolution is designated "S. Res." together with its number. They are considered only by the body in which they were introduced; an adoption is attested to by the Clerk of the House of Representatives or the Secretary of the Senate, as the case may be, and published in the *Congressional Record*.

INTRODUCTION AND REFERENCE TO COMMITTEE

Any Member in the House of Representatives may introduce a bill at any time while the House is actually sitting by simply placing it in the "hopper" provided for this purpose at the side of the Clerk's desk. He is not required to ask permission to introduce the measure or to make a statement at the time of introduction. The name of the sponsor is endorsed on the bill. Under a recent change in the rules of the House, sponsorship of a public bill is no longer limited to 25 Members, but may be by an unlimited number of Members. On his request, a Member may be added as a sponsor no later than the day the bill is reported to the House. In the Senate, unlimited multiple sponsorship of a bill is also permitted. Occasionally, a Member may insert the words "by request" after his name to indicate that the introduction of the measure is in compliance with the suggestion of some other Member.

In the Senate, a Senator usually introduces a bill or resolution by presenting it to the clerks at the Presiding Officer's desk, without commenting on it from the floor of the Senate. However, a Senator may use a more formal procedure by rising and introducing the bill or resolution from the floor. A Senator usually makes a statement about the measure when introducing it on the floor. Frequently, Senators obtain consent to have the bill or resolution printed in the body of the *Congressional Record*, following their formal statement.

If any Senator objects to the introduction of a bill or resolution, the introduction is postponed until the next day. If there is no objection, the bill is read by title and referred to the appropriate committee.

In the House of Representatives it is no longer the custom to read bills — even by title —at the time of introduction. The title is entered in the House Journal and printed in the *Congressional Record*. The bill is assigned its legislative number by the Clerk and referred to the appropriate committees by the Speaker (the Member elected as presiding Officer of the House) with the assistance of the Parliamentarian. These details appear in the daily issue of the *Congressional Record*. It is then sent to the Government Printing Office where it is printed in its introduced form, and printed copies are available shortly thereafter in the document rooms of both Houses. (See Fig. 1, p. 34).

One copy is sent to the office of the chairman of the committee to which it has been referred, for action by that committee. The clerk of the committee enters it on the committee's Legislative Calendar.

Perhaps the most important phase of the Congress process is the action by Committees. This is where the most intensive consideration is given to the proposed measures and where interested members of the public are given an opportunity to be heard.

There are, at present, 22 standing (permanent) committees in the House and 15 in the Senate, as well as several select (special) committees. In the House there are two permanent select committees, the newer being the Permanent Select Committee on Intelligence established in 1977. In addition, there are several standing joint committees of the two Houses, two of which are the Joint Committee on Taxation and the Joint Economic Committee. Select committees are generally of an investigative character and do not consider pending legislation. (See section below entitled "Directory Information" for listing of Senate and House committees.)

Each committee has jurisdiction over certain subject matters of legislation. For example, the House Committee on the Judiciary has jurisdiction over measures relating to judicial proceedings, civil and criminal, and 18 other categories, of which Constitutional amendments, revision and codification of statutes, civil liberties, antitrust, patents, copyrights and trademarks, are but a few. In all, the rules provide for approximately 220 different classifications of measures that are to be referred to the respective committees in the House and nearly 200 in the Senate.

Membership on the various House committees is divided between the two major political parties in proportion to their total membership in the House, except that one-half of the Members on the Committee on Standards of Official Conduct are from the majority party and one-half from the minority party. Until 1953, with certain exceptions, a Member could not serve on more than one standing committee of the House. This limitation was removed, and now all Members may serve on more than one committee. Similar rules prevail in the Senate.

A Member usually seeks election to the committee that has jurisdiction over a field in which he is most qualified and interested. Many Members are nationally recognized experts in the specialty of their particular committee or subcommittee.

Members rank in seniority in accordance with the order of their appointment to the committee, and until recently the ranking majority Member was elected chairman. The rules of the House now require that committee chairmen be elected from nominations submitted by the majority party caucus at the commencement of each Congress.

Most committees have two or more subcommittees that, in addition to having general jurisdiction, specialize in the consideration of particular classifications of bills. For example, the House Committee on Banking, Finance and Urban Affairs has subcommittees that specialize in Financial Regulation and Insurance, Consumer Affairs and Coinage, and Domestic Monetary Policy.

Each committee is provided with a professional and clerical staff. For the standing committees, the professional staff (consisting of not more than eighteen, six of whom may be selected by the minority) is appointed on a permanent basis. The clerical staff (consisting of not more than twelve, four of whom may be selected by the minority) is appointed to handle correspondence and stenographic work. All staff appointments are made by a majority vote of the committee.

Under certain conditions, a standing committee may appoint consultants on a temporary or intermittent basis and may also provide financial assistance to members of its professional staff for the purpose of acquiring specialized training.

CONSIDERATION BY COMMITTEE

Under House rules, the chairman of the committee to which a bill has been referred must refer the bill to the appropriate subcommittee within 2 weeks, unless a majority of the members of the majority party on the committee vote to have the bill considered by the full committee. One of the first actions taken is the transmittal of copies of the bill to the departments and agencies concerned with the subject matter of the measure with a request for their views on the necessity or desirability of enacting the bill into law.

COMMITTEE MEETINGS

Standing committees are required to have regular meeting days no less frequently than once a month, but the chairman may call and convene additional meetings. Three or more members of a standing committee may file with the committee a written request that the chairman call a special meeting. The request must specify the measure or matter to be considered. If the chairman fails, within three calendar days after the filing of the request, to call the requested special meeting, a majority of the members of the committee may call the special meeting by filing with the committee written notice specifying the time and date of the meeting and the measure or matter to be considered.

PUBLIC HEARINGS

If the bill is of sufficient importance, and particularly if it is controversial, the committee will usually set a date for public hearings. Each committee (except the Committee on Rules) is required to make public announcement of the date, place, and subject matter of any hearing at least one week before the commencement of that hearing, unless the committee determines that there is good cause to begin the hearing at an earlier date. If the committee makes that determination, it must make a public announcement to that effect at the earliest possible date. Public announcements are published in the Daily Digest portion of the *Congressional Record*[1] as soon as possible after the announcement is made by the committee, and are often noted in newspapers and periodicals. Personal notice, usually in the form of a letter, but possibly in the form of a subpoena, is sent frequently to individuals, organizations, and Government departments and agencies that are known to be interested.

Committee and subcommittee hearings are required to be public except when the committee or subcommittee, in open session and with a majority present, determines by roll call vote that all or part of that hearing shall be closed to the public, because disclosure of testimony, evidence, or other matters to be considered would endanger the national security or would violate a law or Rule of the House of Representatives.

The bill may be read in full at the opening of the hearings. After a brief introductory statement by the chairman and often by the ranking minority Member or other committee Member, the first witness is called. Cabinet officers and high-ranking civil and military officials of the Government, as well as any private individual who is interested, may appear and testify either voluntarily or at the request or summons (subpoena) of the committee.

Committees require, so far as practicable, that witnesses who appear before it file with the committee, in advance of their appearance, a written statement of their proposed testimony and limit their oral presentations to a brief summary of their arguments.

Minority party Members of the committee are entitled to call witnesses of their own to testify on a measure during at least one day of the hearing.

---

[1]See below, page 30, for a discussion of the *Congressional Record*.

House rules provide that each Member shall have only five minutes in the interrogation of witnesses until each Member of the committee who desires to question a witness has had an opportunity to do so.

A typewritten transcript of the testimony taken at a public hearing is made available for inspection in the office of the clerk of the committee and frequently the complete transcript is printed and distributed by the committee.

BUSINESS MEETINGS

After hearings are completed, the subcommittee usually will consider the bill in a session that is popularly known as the "mark-up" session. The views of both sides are studied in detail and at the conclusion of deliberation a vote is taken to determine the action of the subcommittee. It may decide to report the bill favorably to the full committee, with or without amendment, or unfavorably, or suggest that the committee "table" it, that is, postpone action indefinitely. Each Member of the subcommittee, regardless of party affiliation, has one vote.

All meetings for the transaction of business, including the markup of legislation, must be open to the public except when the committee or subcommittee, in open session with a majority present, determines by roll call vote that all or part of the meeting shall be closed. Members of the committee may, however, authorize congressional staff and departmental representatives to be present at any business or mark-up session that has been so closed.

COMMITTEE ACTION

At meetings of the full committee, reports on bills may be made by subcommittees. Reports are fully discussed and amendments may be offered. Committee amendments are only proposals to change the bill as introduced and are subject to acceptance or rejection by the House itself. A vote of committee Members is taken to determine the action of the full committee on the bill; this action is usually either to report the bill favorably to the House, with or without amendments, or to table it. Because tabling a bill is normally effective in preventing action on it, adverse reports to the House by the full committee are not ordinarily made. On rare occasions, a committee may report a bill without recommendation.

Generally, a majority of the committee constitutes a quorum, i.e., the number of Members who must be present in order for the committee to act. This ensures adequate participation by both sides in the action taken. The rules, however, allow committees to vary the number of Members necessary for a quorum for certain actions. For example, each committee may fix the number of its Members, but not less than two, necessary for a quorum for taking testimony and receiving evidence. The absence of a quorum may be the subject of a point of order — that is, an objection that the proceedings are out of order.

PUBLIC INSPECTION OF RESULTS OF ROLL CALL VOTE IN COMMITTEE

The result of each roll call vote in any meeting of a committee must be made available by that committee for inspection by the public. Information available for public inspection includes a description of each amendment, motion, order, or other proposition; the name of each Member voting for and each Member voting against the amendment, motion, order, or proposition, and whether by proxy or in person; and the names of those Members present but not voting.

With respect to each roll call vote by a committee on a motion to report a bill or resolution, the total number of votes cast for, and the total number of votes cast against, the reporting of the bill or resolution must be included in the committee report.

PROXY VOTING

A vote by a Member of a committee with respect to a measure or other matter may not be cast by proxy unless that committee adopts a written rule that permits voting by proxy and requires that the proxy authorization (1) be in writing, (2) assert that the Member is absent on official business or is otherwise unable to be present at the meeting of the committee, (3) designate the person who is to execute the proxy authorization, and (4) be limited to a specific measure or matter and any amendments or motions pertaining to the measure or matter. A Member may authorize a "general proxy" only for motions to recess, adjourn or other procedural matters. A proxy must be signed by the Member and must contain the date and time of day that it is signed. A proxy may not be counted for a quorum.

REPORTED BILLS

If the committee votes to report the bill favorably to the House, one of the Members is designated to write the committee report. The report describes the purpose and scope of the bill and the reasons for its recommended approval. Generally, a section-by-section analysis is set forth in detail explaining precisely what each section is intended to accomplish. Under the rules of the House, all changes in existing law must be indicated and the text of laws being repealed must be set out. Committee amendments must also be set out at the beginning of the report and explanations of them included. Executive communications requesting the introduction and consideration of the bill, if applicable, are usually quoted in full.

If at the time of approval of a bill by a committee a Member of the committee gives notice of his intention to file supplemental, minority, or additional views, that Member is entitled to not less than three calendar days (Saturdays, Sundays, and legal holidays excluded) in which to file those views with the clerk of the committee and they must be included in the report on the bill.

The report is assigned a report number when it is filed, and it is delivered to the Government Printing Office for printing. The report number contains a prefix-designator which indicates the number of the Congress. For example, the first House report for the 97th Congress (1981-82), was numbered 97-1.

The bill also is printed when reported (see Fig. 2, p. 35) and committee amendments are indicated by showing new matter in italics and any deleted matter in stricken-through type. The report number is also printed on the bill and the calendar number is shown on both the first and back pages of the bill. (See "Calendar" section below, p. 13.)

Committee reports (see Fig. 3, p 36) are perhaps the most valuable single element of the legislative history of a law. They are used by the courts, executive departments and agencies, and the public generally, as a source of information regarding the purpose and meaning of the legislation.

CONTENTS OF REPORTS

The report of a committee on a measure that it has approved must include: (A) the committee's oversight findings and recommendations, (B) the statement required by the Congressional Budget Act of 1974, if the measure provides new budget authority or new or increased expenditures, (C) the estimate and comparison prepared by the Director of the Congressional Budget Office whenever the Director has submitted such to the committee prior to the filing of the report, and (D) a summary of the oversight findings and recommendations made by the Committee on Government Operations if such have been submitted in a timely fashion. Each of these items is separately set out and clearly identified in the report.

INFLATIONARY IMPACT AND COST ESTIMATES IN REPORTS

Each report of a committee on a bill or joint resolution reported by the committee must contain a detailed analytical statement as to whether the enactment of the bill or joint resolution into law may have an inflationary impact on prices and costs in the national economy.

Each report also must contain an estimate, made by the committee, of the costs which would be incurred in carrying out that bill or joint resolution in the fiscal year reported and in each of the 5 fiscal years thereafter or for the duration of the program authorized if less than 5 years. In the case of a measure involving revenues, the report need contain only an estimate of the gain or loss in revenues for a 1-year period. The report must also include a comparison of the estimates of those costs with the estimate made by any Government agency and submitted to that committee. The Committees on Appropriations are not required to include cost estimates in their reports.

FILING OF REPORTS

Measures approved by a committee must be reported promptly after approval. A majority of the Members of the committee may file a written request with the clerk of the committee for the reporting of the measure. When the request is filed, the clerk immediately must notify the chairman of the committee of the filing of the request, and the report on the measure must be filed within seven days (exclusive of days on which the House is not in session) after the day on which the request is filed. This does not apply to the reporting of a regular appropriations bill by the Committee on Appropriations prior to compliance with requirements set out in the next paragraph.

Before reporting the first regular appropriation bill for each fiscal year, the Committee on Appropriations must, to the extent practicable and in accordance with the Congressional Budget Act of 1974, complete subcommittee markup and full committee action on all regular appropriation bills for that year and submit to the House a summary report comparing the Committee's recommendations with the appropriate levels of budget outlays and new budget authority as set forth in the most recently agreed to concurrent resolution on the budget for that year. (See Part II below for discussion of the budget process.)

Generally, bills or resolutions that directly or indirectly authorize the enactment of new budget authority for a fiscal year must be reported to the House on or before May 15 preceding the beginning of that fiscal year. This deadline may be waived in emergency situations.

AVAILABILITY OF REPORTS AND HEARINGS

With certain exceptions, a measure reported by a committee may not be considered in the House until the third calendar day (excluding Saturdays, Sundays, and legal holidays) on which the committee report on that measure has been available to the Members of the House. If hearings were held on a measure so reported, the committee is required to make every reasonable effort to have those hearings printed and available for distribution to the Members of the House prior to the consideration of the measure in the House. General appropriation bills may not be considered until printed committee hearings and a committee report thereon have been available to the Members of the House for at least three calendar days.

LEGISLATIVE REVIEW BY STANDING COMMITTEES

Under the rules of the House, each standing committee (other than the Committees on Appropriations, and on the Budget) is required to review and study, on a continuing basis, the application, administration, execution, and effectiveness of the laws dealing with the subject matter over which the committee has jurisdiction and the operation of Federal agencies having responsibility for the administration and evaluation of those laws.

The purpose of the review and study is to determine whether laws and the programs created by Congress are being carried out in accordance with the intent of Congress and whether those programs should be continued, curtailed, or eliminated. Each committee having oversight responsibility is required to review any conditions or circumstances that may indicate the necessity or desirability of enacting new or additional legislation within the jurisdiction of that committee. Each standing committee also has the function of reviewing and studying, on a continuing basis, the impact of tax policies on matters within its jurisdiction.

At the beginning of each Congress, a representative of the Committee on Government Operations meets with representatives of each of the other committees of the House to discuss the oversight plans of those committees and to assist in coordinating all of the oversight activities of the House during that Congress. Within 60 days after Congress convenes, the committee reports to the House the results of those meetings and discussions, and any recommendations which it has to assure the most effective coordination of oversight activities and otherwise achieve the oversight objectives.

CALENDARS

A calendar of the House of Representatives, together with a history of all measures reported by a standing committee of either House, is printed each day the House is sitting, for the information of those interested.

As soon as a bill is favorably reported, it is assigned a calendar number on either the Union Calendar or the House Calendar (see below), the two principal calendars of business. The calendar number is printed on both the first and the back pages of the bill. In the case of a bill that was referred to two or more committees for consideration in sequence, the calendar number is printed only on the bill as reported by the last committee to consider it.

UNION CALENDAR

The rules of the House provide that there shall be:

First. A Calendar of the Committee of the Whole House on the state of the Union, to which shall be referred bills raising revenue, general appropriation bills, and bills of a public character directly or indirectly appropriating money or property.

This is commonly known as the Union Calendar and the large majority of public bills and resolutions are placed on it upon being reported to the House.

HOUSE CALENDAR

The rules further provide that there shall be:

Second. A House Calendar, to which shall be referred all bills of a public character not raising revenue nor directly or indirectly appropriating money or property.

Public bills and resolutions that are not placed on the Union Calendar are referred to the House Calendar.

CONSENT CALENDAR

If a measure pending on either of these calendars is of a noncontroversial nature, it may be placed on the Consent Calendar. The House rules provide that after a bill has been favorably reported and is on either the House or Union Calendar, any Member may file with the Clerk a notice that he desires the bill placed on the Consent Calendar. On the first and third Mondays of each month immediately after the reading of the Journal, the Speaker directs the Clerk to call the bills in numerical order that have been on the Consent Calendar for three legislative days. If objection is made to the consideration of any bill so called it is carried over on the calendar without prejudice to the next day when the Consent Calendar is again called, and if then objected to by three or more Members it is immediately stricken from the calendar and may not be placed on the Consent Calendar again during that session of Congress. If objection is not made and if the bill is not "passed over" by request, it is passed by unanimous consent without debate. Ordinarily the only amendments considered are those sponsored by the committee that reported the bill.

To avoid the passage without debate of measures that may be controversial or are sufficiently important or complex to require full discussion, there are six official objectors — three on the majority side and three on the minority side — who make a careful study of bills on the Consent Calendar. If a bill involves the expenditure of more than a fixed sum of money or if it changes national policy or has other aspects that any of the objectors believes demand explanation and debate, it will be objected to and will not be passed by consent. That action does not necessarily mean the final defeat of the bill, since it may then be brought up for consideration in the same way as any other bill on the House or Union Calendars. This will be discussed next, after a look at the Private Calendar.

PRIVATE CALENDAR

All bills of a private character, that is, bills that affect an individual rather than the population at large, are called private bills. A private bill is used for relief in matters such as immigration and naturalization and claims by or against the United States. A private bill is referred to the Private Calendar. That calendar is called on the first and third Tuesdays of each month. If objection is made by two or more Members to the consideration of any measure called, it is recommitted to the committee that reported it. As in the case of the Consent Calendar there are six official objectors, three on the majority side and three on the minority side, who make a careful study of each bill or resolution on the Private Calendar and who will object to a measure that does not conform to the requirements for that calendar.

OBTAINING CONSIDERATION OF MEASURES

Certain measures pending on the House and Union Calendars are, obviously, more important and urgent than others, and it is necessary to have a system permitting their consideration ahead of those that do not require immediate action. Because all measures are placed on those calendars in the order in which they are reported to the House, the latest bill reported would be the last to be taken up if calendar number alone were the determining factor.

SPECIAL RESOLUTIONS

To avoid delays and to provide some degree of selectivity in the consideration of measures, it is possible to have them taken up out of order by procuring from the Committee on Rules a special resolution or "rule" for their consideration. That committee, which is composed of majority and minority Members (but with a larger portion of majority Members than other committees), is specifically granted jurisdiction over resolutions relating to the order of business of the House. Usually the chairman of the committee that has favorably reported the bill appears before the Committee on Rules accompanied by the sponsor of the measure and one or more members of his committee in support of his request for a resolution providing for its immediate consideration. If the Rules Committee is satisfied that the measure should be taken up, it will report a resolution reading substantially as follows with respect to a bill on the Union Calendar:

> *Resolved,* That upon the adoption of this resolution it shall be in order to move that the House resolve itself into the Committee of the Whole House on the State of the Union for the consideration of the bill (H.R.____) entitled, etc., and the first reading of the bill shall be dispensed with. After general debate, which shall be confined to the bill and shall continue not to exceed ____ hours, to be equally divided and controlled by the chairman and ranking minority member of the Committee on ____, the bill shall be read for amendment under the five-minute rule. At the conclusion of the consideration of the bill for amendment, the Committee shall rise and report the bill to the House with such amendments as may have been adopted, and the previous question[1] shall be considered as ordered on the bill and amendments thereto to final passage without intervening motion except one motion to recommit.

The resolution may waive points of order against the bill. When it limits or prevents floor amendments, it is popularly known as a "closed rule".

CONSIDERATION OF MEASURES MADE IN ORDER BY PREVIOUS RESOLUTION

When a "rule" has been reported to the House, and is not considered immediately, it is referred to the calendar. If not called up for consideration by the Member of the Rules Committee who made the report, within 7 legislative days thereafter, any member of the Rules Committee may call it up as a question of privilege.

Also, if within 7 calendar days after a measure has, by resolution, been made in order for consideration by the House, a motion has not been offered for its consideration, the Speaker may, in his discretion, recognize a Member of the committee that reported the measure to offer a motion that the House consider it, if the Member has been duly authorized by that committee to offer the motion.

There are several other methods of obtaining consideration of bills that either have not been reported by a committee or, if reported, for which a special resolution or "rule" has not been obtained. These methods include: "Motion to Suspend the Rules," "Calender Wednesday," and "Privileged Matters."

MOTION TO SUSPEND THE RULES

On Monday and Tuesday of each week and during the last 6 days of a session, the Speaker may entertain a motion to suspend the operation of the regular rules and pass a bill or resolution. Arrangement must be made in advance with the Speaker to recognize the Member who wishes to offer the motion. Before being considered by the House, the motion must be seconded by a majority of the Members present. A second, however, is not required on a motion to suspend the rules when printed copies of the proposed bill or resolution have been available for one legislative day before the motion is considered. The motion to suspend the rules and pass the bill is then debated for 40 minutes, one-half by those in favor of the proposition and one-half by those opposed. The motion may not be amended, and if amendments to the bill are proposed they must be included in the motion when it is made. The rules may be suspended and the bill passed only by affirmative vote of two-thirds of the Members voting, a quorum being present.

---

[1]The "previous question" is a method for cutting off debate. See section below entitled "Action by the House," page 18.

CALENDAR WEDNESDAY

On Wednesday of each week, unless dispensed with by unanimous consent or by affirmative vote of two-thirds of the Members voting, a quorum being present, the standing committees are called in alphabetical order. A committee when named may call up for consideration any bill reported by it on a previous day and pending on either the House or Union Calendar. Not more than two hours of general debate is permitted on any measure called up on Calendar Wednesday, and all debate must be confined to the subject matter of the measure, the time being equally divided between those for and those against it. The affirmative vote of a simple majority of the Members present is sufficient to pass the measure.

PRIVILEGED MATTERS

Under the rules of the House, certain matters are regarded as privileged matters and may interrupt the order of business; for example, reports from the Committee on Rules and reports from the Committee on Appropriations on the general appropriation bills.

At any time after the reading of the Journal, a Member, by direction of the appropriate committee, may move that the House resolve itself into the Committee of the Whole House on the State of the Union for the purpose of considering bills raising revenues, or general appropriation bills. General appropriation bills may not be considered in the House until three calendar days (excluding Saturdays, Sundays, and legal holidays) after printed committee reports and hearings on them have been available to the Members. The limit on general debate is generally fixed by unanimous consent.

Other examples of privileged matters are conference reports, certain amendments to measures by the Senate, veto messages from the President of the United States, and resolutions privileged pursuant to statute. The Member in charge of such a matter may call it up at practically any time for immediate consideration. Usually, this is done after consultation with both the majority and minority floor leaders so that the Members of both parties will have advance notice and not be taken by surprise.

CONSIDERATION

Once consideration of a measure is obtained by one of the methods discussed above, our legislative tradition demands that it be given consideration by the entire membership with adequate opportunity for debate and the offering of amendments.[1]

COMMITTEE OF THE WHOLE HOUSE

In order to expedite the consideration of bills and resolutions, the House resorts to a parliamentary usage that enables it to act with a quorum of only 100 Members instead of the normally requisite majority of 218 (of the 435 total membership). This consists of resolving itself into the Committee of the Whole House on the State of the Union to consider a measure. All measures on the Union Calendar — involving a tax, appropriations, or authorizing payments out of appropriations already made — must be first considered in the Committee of the Whole.

Members debate and vote on the motion that the House resolve itself into the Committee of the Whole. If the motion is adopted, the Speaker leaves his chair after appointing a Chairman to preside.

---

[1] The discussion to follow will focus on House procedures for obtaining consideration of a measure. A brief look at Senate procedure begins below on page 21.

The special resolution or "rule" reported by the Committee on Rules to allow for immediate consideration of the measure fixes the length of the debate in the Committee of the Whole. This may vary according to the importance and controversial nature of the measure. As provided in the resolution, the control of the time is divided equally — usually between the Chairman and the ranking minority Member of the committee that reported the measure. Members seeking to speak for or against the measure usually make arrangements in advance with the Member in control of the time on their respective side. Others may ask the Member speaking at the time to yield to them for a question or a brief statement. Frequently permission is granted a Member by unanimous consent to extend his remarks in the *Congressional Record* if sufficient time to make a lengthy oral statement is not available during actual debate.

The conduct of the debate is governed principally by the standing rules of the House that are adopted at the opening of each Congress. Another recognized authority is Jefferson's Manual that was prepared by Thomas Jefferson for his own guidance as President of the Senate from 1797 to 1801. The House, in 1837, adopted a rule that still stands, providing that the provisions of Jefferson's Manual should govern the House in all cases to which they are applicable and in which they are not inconsistent with the standing rules and orders of the House.

SECOND READING

During the general debate an accurate account is kept of the time used on both sides, and when all the time allowed under the rule has been consumed the Chairman terminates the debate. Then begins the "second reading of the bill", section by section, at which time amendments may be offered to a section when it is read. Under the House rules, a Member is permitted five minutes to explain his proposed amendment, after which the Member who is first recognized by the Chair is allowed to speak for five minutes in opposition to it; there is no further debate on that amendment, thereby effectively preventing any attempt at filibuster tactics. This is known as the "five-minute rule". There is, however, a device whereby a Member may offer a pro forma amendment — "to strike out the last word" — without intending any change in the language, and be allowed five minutes for debate, thus permitting a somewhat more comprehensive debate. Each amendment (except a *pro forma* amendment) is put to the Committee of the Whole for adoption.

At any time after debate is begun under the five-minute rule on proposed amendments to a section or paragraph of a bill, the Committee of the Whole may, by majority vote of the Members present, close debate on the section or paragraph. If, however, debate is closed on a section or paragraph before there has been debate on any amendment that a Member has caused to be printed in the *Congressional Record* after the reporting of the bill by the committee but at least one day prior to floor consideration of the amendment, the Member who caused the amendment to be printed in the *Record* is given five minutes in which to explain the amendment, after which the first person to obtain the floor has five minutes to speak in opposition to it, and there is no further debate on that proposed amendment; but time for debate is not allowed when the offering of the amendment is dilatory.

THE COMMITTEE "RISES"

At the conclusion of the consideration of a bill for amendment, the Committee of the Whole "rises" and reports the bill to the House with the amendments that have been adopted. In rising, the Committee of the Whole reverts back to the House and the Chairman of the Committee is replaced in the chair by the Speaker of the House. The House then acts on the bill and any amendments adopted by the Committee of the Whole.

ACTION BY THE HOUSE

Under the rules of the House, debate is cut off by moving "the previous question". If this motion is carried by a majority of the Members voting, a quorum being present, all debate is cut off on the bill on which the previous question has been ordered. The Speaker then puts the question: "Shall the bill be engrossed and read a third time?" If this question is decided in the affirmative, the bill is read a third time by title only and voted on for passage.

If the previous question has been ordered by the terms of the special resolution or "rule" on a bill reported by the Committee of the Whole, the House immediately votes on whatever amendments have been reported by the Committee in the sequence in which they were reported. After completion of voting on the amendments, the House immediately votes on the passage of the bill with any amendments it has adopted.

In those cases where the previous question has not been ordered, the House may engage in debate lasting one hour, at the conclusion of which the previous question is ordered and the House votes on the passage of the bill. During the debate it is in order to offer amendments to the bill or to the Committee amendments.

In 1979, the House amended its rules to allow the Speaker to postpone a vote on final passage of a bill or resolution or agreement to a conference report. A vote may be postponed for up to two legislative days.

Measures that do not have to be considered in the Committee of the Whole are considered in the House in the first instance under the hour rule or in accordance with the terms of the special resolution limiting debate on the measure.

After passage of the bill by the House, a *pro forma* motion to reconsider it is automatically made and laid on the table. The purpose of this action is to forestall such a motion at a later date, because the vote of the House on a proposition is not final and conclusive on the House until there has been an opportunity to reconsider it.

MOTIONS TO RECOMMIT

After the previous question has been ordered on the passage of a bill or joint resolution, it is in order to make one motion to recommit the bill or joint resolution to a committee, and the Speaker is required to give preference in recognition for that purpose to a Member who is opposed to the bill or joint resolution. This motion is normally not subject to debate. However, with respect to a motion to "recommit" with instructions" after the previous question has been ordered, a ten minute debate is in order before the vote is taken, the time to be equally divided between the proponents and opponents of the motion.

QUORUM CALLS AND ROLL CALLS

In order to speed up and expedite quorum calls and roll calls, the rules of the House provide alternative methods for pursuing these procedures.

The rules provide that in the absence of a quorum, fifteen Members, including the Speaker, are authorized to compel the attendance of absent Members. A call of the House is then ordered, and the Speaker is required to have the call taken by electronic device, unless in his discretion he names one or more clerks "to tell" the Members who are present. In that case the names of those present are recorded by the clerks, and entered in the Journal of the House and absent Members have not less than 15 minutes from the ordering of the call of the House to have their presence recorded. If sufficient excuse is not offered for their absence, by order of a majority of those present, they may be sent for by officers appointed by the Sergeant-at-Arms for that purpose, and their attendance secured and retained. The House then determines the conditions on which they may be discharged. Members who voluntarily appear are, unless the House otherwise directs, immediately admitted to the Hall of the House and they must report their names to the Clerk to be entered in the Journal as present.

At any time after the roll call has been completed, the Speaker may entertain a motion to adjourn, if seconded by a majority of those present as ascertained by actual count by the Speaker; and if the House adjourns, all proceedings as herein described are vacated.

House rules prohibit quorum calls on such occasions as before or during the daily prayer, during administration of the oath of office to the Speaker or any Member, during the reception of messages from the President or the Senate, or in connection with motions incidental to a call of the House.

The first time the Committee of the Whole finds itself without a quorum during any day, the Chairman is required to order the roll to be called by electronic device, unless, in his discretion, he orders a call by naming clerks "to tell" the Members, as described above. If on a call a quorum appears, the Committee continues its business. If a quorum does not appear, the Committee rises and the Chairman reports the names of the absentees to the House. The House rules provide for the expeditious conduct of quorum calls in the Committee of the Whole. The Chairman may suspend a quorum call once he or she determines that a bare or minimum quorum has been reached, that is, 100 or more Members. Under such a short quorum call, the Committee will not rise, and therefore Members' names will not be published. Once the presence of a quorum of the Committee of the Whole has been established for the day, quorum calls in the Committee are only in order when the Committee is operating under the five-minute rule and the Chairman has put the pending motion or proposition to a vote.

VOTING

There are four methods of voting in the Committee of the Whole. These are the voice vote (viva voce), the division, the teller vote, and the recorded vote. An additional method, the yea-and-nay vote, is used only in the House when not resolved into the Committee of the Whole. If a Member objects to the vote on the ground that a quorum is not present in the House, there may be an automatic roll call vote.

To obtain a voice vote the Chair states, "As many as are in favor of (as the question may be) say 'Aye'." "As many as are opposed, say 'No'." The Chair determines the result on the basis of the volume of ayes and noes. This is the form in which the vote is ordinarily taken in the first instance.

If it is difficult to determine the result of a voice vote, a division may be demanded. The Chair then states that a division has been demanded and says "as many as are in favor will rise and stand until counted". After counting those in favor he calls on those opposed to stand and be counted, thereby determining the number in favor of and those opposed to the question.

If a demand for a teller vote is supported by one-fifth of a quorum (20 in the Committee of the Whole, and 44 in the House), the Chair appoints one or more tellers from each side and directs the Members in favor of the proposition to pass between the tellers and be counted. After counting, a teller announces the number in the affirmative, and the Chair then directs the Members opposed to pass between the tellers and be counted. When the count is stated by a teller, the Chair announces the result.

If any Member requests a recorded vote and that request is supported by at least one-fifth of a quorum of the House, or 25 Members in the Committee of the Whole, the vote is taken by electronic device, unless the Speaker, in his discretion, orders clerks "to tell", that is, record the names of those voting on each side of the question. After the recorded vote is concluded, the names of those voting together with those not voting are entered in the Journal. Members usually have fifteen minutes to be counted from the time the recorded vote is ordered or the ordering of the clerks "to tell" the vote. The House rules, however, allow the Speaker, in certain situations, to reduce the period for voting to five minutes.

In addition to the foregoing methods of voting, if the yeas and nays are demanded, the Speaker directs those in favor of taking the vote by that method to stand and be counted. The assent of one-fifth of the Members present (as distinguished from one-fifth of a quorum in the case of a demand for tellers) is necessary for ordering the yeas and nays. When the yeas and nays are ordered (or a point of order is made that a quorum is not present) the Speaker directs that as many as are in favor of the proposition will, as their names are called, answer "Aye"; as many as are opposed will answer "No". The Clerk calls the roll and reports the result to the Speaker who announces it to the House. The Speaker is not required to vote unless his vote would be decisive.

ELECTRONIC VOTING

Under modern practice, recorded and roll call votes are usually taken by electronic device, except when the Speaker, in his discretion, orders the vote to be recorded by other methods prescribed by the rules of the House, and in emergency situations, such as the failure of the electronic device to function. In addition, quorum calls are generally taken by electronic device. Essentially the system works as follows: A number of vote stations are attached to selected chairs in the Chamber. Each station is equipped with a vote card slot and four indicators, marked "yea", "nay", "present", and "open". The "open" indicator is used only when a vote is in progress and the system is ready to accept votes. Each Member is furnished with a personalized Vote-ID Card. A Member casts his vote by inserting his card into any one of the vote stations and depressing the appropriate push button indicator according to his choice. The machine records the votes and reports the result when the vote is completed. In the event the Member finds himself without his Vote-ID Card, he may still cast his vote by paper ballot, which he hands to the Tally Clerk, who may then record the vote electronically according to the indicated preference of the Member. The paper ballots are green for "yea", red for "nay", and amber for "present".

PAIRING OF MEMBERS

When a Member anticipates that he will be unavoidably absent at the time a vote is to be taken, he may arrange in advance to be recorded as being either in favor of, or opposed to, the question by being "paired" with a Member who will also be absent and who holds contrary views on the question. A specific pair of this kind shows how he would have voted if he had been present. Occasionally, a Member who has arranged in advance to be paired actually is present at the time of voting. He then votes as he would have voted if he had not been paired, and subsequently withdraws his vote and asks to be marked "present" to protect his colleague. This is known as a "live pair". If his absence is to continue for several days during which a number of different questions are to be voted upon, he may arrange a "general pair". A general pair does not indicate how he would have voted on the question, but merely that he and the Member paired with him would not have been on the same side of the question.

Pairs are not counted in determining the vote on the question, but, rather, provide an opportunity for absent Members to express formally how they would have voted had they been present. Pairs are announced by the Clerk of the House and are listed in the *Congressional Record* immediately after the names of those Members not voting on the question.

BROADCASTING LIVE COVERAGE OF FLOOR PROCEEDINGS

Recently, the House amended its rules to provide for unedited audio and visual broadcasting and recording of proceedings on the floor of the House. House rules prohibit the use of these broadcasts and recordings for any political purpose or in any commercial advertisement.

ENGROSSMENT AND MESSAGE TO SENATE

The preparation of a copy of the bill in the form in which it has passed the House is sometimes a detailed and complicated process because of the large number and complexity of amendments that may have been adopted. The amendment may be for the purpose of inserting new language, substituting different words for those set out in the bill, or deleting portions of the bill. It is not unusual to have more than 100 amendments, including those proposed by the committee at the time the bill is reported and those offered from the floor during the consideration of the bill in the chamber. Some of the amendments offered from the floor are written in longhand and others are typewritten. Each amendment must be inserted in precisely the proper place in the bill, with the spelling and punctuation exactly the same as it was adopted by the House. It is extremely important that the Senate receive a copy of the bill in the precise form in which it has passed the House. The preparation of such a copy is the function of the enrolling clerk.

There is an enrolling clerk in both the House and Senate. He receives all the papers relating to the bill, including the official Clerk's copy of the bill as reported by the standing committee and each amendment adopted by the House. From this material he prepares the engrossed copy of the bill as passed, containing all the amendments agreed to by the House. (See Fig. 4, p. 37). At this point the measure ceases technically to be called a bill and is termed "an act" signifying that it is the act of one body of the Congress, although it is still popularly referred to as a bill. The engrossed bill is printed on blue paper and a certificate that it passed the House of Representatives is signed by the Clerk of the House. The engrossed bill is delivered by a reading clerk to the Senate.

SENATE ACTION

The Presiding Officer of the Senate refers the engrossed bill to the appropriate standing committee of the Senate in conformity with the rules. The bill is immediately reprinted and copies are made available in the document rooms of both Houses. (See Fig. 5, p. 38). This printing is known as the "Act print" or the "Senate referred print".

COMMITTEE CONSIDERATION

Senate committees give the bill the same kind of detailed consideration as it received in the House, and may report it with or without amendment, or "table" it (i.e., remove it from consideration). A committee member who wishes to express his individual views, or a group of members who wish to file a minority report, may do so, if he or they give notice at the time of the approval of the measure.

When a committee reports a bill, it is reprinted with the committee amendments indicated by line-through type and italics. The calendar number and report number are indicated on the first and back pages, together with the name of the Senator making the report. (See Fig. 6, p. 39) The committee report and any minority or individual views accompanying the bill also are printed at the same time. (See Fig. 7, p. 40) Any Senator may enter a motion to discharge a committee from further consideration of a bill that it has failed to report after what is deemed a reasonable time. If the motion is agreed to by a majority vote, the committee is discharged and the bill is placed on the Calendar of Business under the standing rules. (See below).

All committee meetings, including those to conduct hearings, must be open to the public. A majority of the members of a committee or subcommittee may, however, after discussion in closed session, vote in open session to close a meeting or series of meetings on the same subject for no longer than 14 days if it is determined that the matters to be discussed, or testimony to be taken: will disclose matters necessary to be kept secret in the interests of national defense or the confidential conduct of the foreign relations of the United States; relate solely to internal committee staff management or procedure; tend to reflect adversely on the reputation of an individual or may represent an unwarranted invasion of the privacy of an individual; may disclose law enforcement information that is required to be kept secret; may disclose certain information regarding certain trade secrets; or may disclose matters required to be kept confidential under other provisions of law or Government regulation.

CHAMBER PROCEDURE

The rules of procedure in the Senate differ considerably from those in the House. At the time that a bill is reported, the Senator who is making the report may ask unanimous consent for the immediate consideration of the bill. If the bill is of a noncontroversial nature and there is no objection, the Senate may pass the bill with little or no debate and with only a brief explanation of its purpose and effect. The bill, however, is subject to amendment by any Senator. A simple majority vote is necessary to carry an amendment as well as to pass the bill. If there is any objection, the report must lie over one day and the bill is placed on the calendar.

Measures reported by standing committees of the Senate may not be considered unless the report of that committee has been available to Senate Members for at least three days (excluding Saturdays, Sundays, and legal holidays) prior to consideration of the measure in the Senate. This requirement, however, may be waived by agreement of the majority and minority leaders and does not apply in certain emergency situations.

Measures typically are passed by the Senate either on a motion to consider a measure on the calendar or under a unanimous consent order. A unanimous consent order often limits the amount of debate that will take place and lists the amendments that will be considered. Usually a motion to consider a measure on the calendar is made only when unanimous consent to consider the measure cannot be obtained.

There is only one Calendar of Business in the Senate, there being no differentiation (as there is in the House) between (1) bills raising revenue, general appropriation bills, and bills of a public character appropriating money or property, and (2) other bills of a public character not appropriating money or property.

The Senate rules provide that at the conclusion of the morning business for each legislative day, the Senate proceeds to the consideration of the Calendar of Business. Under modern practice, however, this rule is usually waived by unanimous consent and it is rare to have a call of the calendar. When the calendar is called, bills that are not objected to are taken up in their order, and each Senator is entitled to speak once (and for five minutes only) on any question. Objection may be interposed at any stage of the proceedings, but on motion, the Senate may continue consideration after the call of the calendar is completed, and the limitations on debate then do not apply.

On any day but Monday, following the announcement of the close of morning business, any Senator obtaining recognition, usually the majority leader, may move to take up any bill out of its regular order on the calendar. The five-minute limitation on debate does not apply to the consideration of a bill taken up in this manner, and debate may continue until the hour when the Presiding Officer of the Senate "lays down" the unfinished business of the day. At that point consideration of the bill is discontinued and the measure reverts back to the Calendar of Business and may again be called up at another time under the same conditions.

When a bill has been objected to and passed over on the call of the calendar, it is not necessarily lost. The majority leader, after consulting the majority policy committee of the Senate and the minority leadership, determines the time at which it will be called up for debate. At that time, a motion is made to consider the bill. The motion, which is debatable, if made after the morning hour, is sometimes the occasion for lengthy speeches, on the part of Senators opposed to the measure. This is the tactic known as "filibustering". Upon obtaining the floor, Senators may speak as long as they please but may not speak more than twice on any one question in debate on the same day without leave of the Senate. Debate, however, may be closed if 16 Senators sign a motion to that effect and the motion is carried by three-fifths of the total membership of the Senate. Such a motion is voted on without debate on the second day after the day it is filed. This procedure is called "invoking cloture".

While a measure is being considered it is subject to amendment and each amendment, including those proposed by the committee that reported the bill, is considered separately. Generally there is no requirement that proposed amendments be germane to the subject matter of the bill except in the case of general appropriation bills. Under the rules of the Senate a "rider", that is, an amendment proposing substantive legislation to an appropriation bill is prohibited, but this prohibition may be suspended by two-thirds vote on a motion to permit consideration of such an amendment on one day's notice in writing. After final action on the amendments, the bill is ready for engrossment and the third reading, which is usually by title only.

The Presiding Officer then puts the question on the passage and the vote is usually taken viva voce, although a yea-and-nay vote is in order if demanded by one-fifth of the Senators present. A simple majority is necessary for passage. Before an amended measure is cleared for its return to the House of Representatives (or an unamended measure is cleared for enrollment) a Senator who voted with the prevailing side, or who abstained from voting, may make a motion within the next two days to reconsider the action. If the measure was passed without a recorded vote, any Senator may make the motion to reconsider. That motion is usually tabled and its tabling constitutes a final determination. If, however, the motion is granted, the Senate, by majority vote, may either affirm its action, which then becomes final, or reverse it.

The original engrossed House bill, together with the engrossed Senate amendments, if any, is then returned to the House with a message stating the action taken by the Senate. Where amendments have been made by the Senate, the message requests that the House concur in them.

FINAL ACTION ON AMENDED BILL

On their return to the House, the official papers relating to the amended measure are placed on the Speaker's table to await House action on the Senate amendments. If the amendments are of a minor or noncontroversial nature, the Chairman of the committee that originally reported the bill — or any Member — may, at the direction of the committee, ask unanimous consent to take the bill with the amendments from the Speaker's table and agree to the Senate amendments. At this point the Clerk reads the title of the bill and the Senate amendments. If there is no objection the amendments are then declared to be agreed to, and the bill is ready to be enrolled for presentation to the President. Lacking unanimous consent, bills that do not require consideration in the Committee of the Whole are privileged and may be called up from the Speaker's table by motion for immediate consideration of the amendments. A simple majority is necessary to carry the motion and thereby complete floor action on the measure. A Senate amendment to a House bill is subject to a point of order that it must first be considered in the Committee of the Whole, if, originating in the House, it would be subject to that point.

REQUEST FOR A CONFERENCE

If, however, the amendments are substantial or controversial, the Member may request unanimous consent to take the bill with the Senate amendments from the Speaker's table, disagree to the amendments, and request a conference with the Senate to resolve the disagreeing votes of the two Houses. If there is objection to such request, it becomes necessary to obtain a special resolution from the Committee on Rules unless the Speaker, in his discretion, recognizes a Member for a motion, authorized by the committee having jurisdiction over the subject matter of the bill, to disagree to the amendments and ask for a conference. If there is no objection to the request, or if the motion is carried, the Speaker then appoints the managers (as the conferees are called) on the part of the House and a message is sent to the Senate advising it of the House action.

A majority of the Members appointed to be managers must have been supporters of the House position, as determined by the Speaker. The Speaker must name Members who are primarily responsible for the legislation and must include, to the fullest extent feasible, the principal proponents of the major provisions of the bill as it passed the House. The Speaker usually follows the suggestions of the Chairman of the committee in charge of the bill in designating the managers on the part of the House. The number, as fixed by the Speaker, is frequently seven, consisting of five Members of the majority party and two of the minority, but may be greater on important bills.

If the Senate agrees to the request for a conference, a similar committee is appointed by unanimous consent by the Presiding Officer of the Senate. Both political parties may be represented on the Senate conference committee also, but the Senate committee need not be the same size as the House committee.

The conference committee is sometimes popularly referred to as the "Third House of Congress".

The request for a conference can be made only by the body in possession of the official papers. Occasionally the Senate, anticipating that the House will not concur in its amendments, votes to insist on its amendments and requests a conference on passage of the bill prior to returning the bill to the House. This practice serves to expedite the matter because several days' time may be saved by the designation of the Senate conferees before returning the bill to the House. The matter of which body requests the conference is not without significance, because the one asking for the conference acts last on the report to be submitted by the conferees.

AUTHORITY OF CONFEREES

Although the managers on the part of each House meet together as one committee, they are in effect two separate committees, each of which votes separately and acts by a majority vote. For this reason the number of the respective managers (conferees) is largely immaterial.

The conferees are strictly limited in their consideration to matters in disagreement between the two Houses. Consequently they may not strike out or amend any portion of the bill that was not amended by the Senate. Furthermore, they may not insert new matter that is not germane to the differences between the two Houses. Where the Senate amendment revises a figure or an amount contained in the bill, the conferees are limited to the difference between the two numbers and may not increase the greater nor decrease the smaller figure. Neither House alone may, by instructions, empower its managers to make a change in the text to which both Houses have agreed, but the managers for both bodies may be given that authority by a concurrent resolution adopted by a majority of each House.

When a disagreement to an amendment in the nature of a substitute is committed to a conference committee, it is in order for the managers on the part of the House to propose a substitute which is a germane modification of the matter in disagreement; but the introduction of language in that substitute presenting an additional topic or issue not committed to the conference committee by either House does not constitute a germane modification of the matter in disagreement.

An amendment by the Senate to a general appropriation bill which would be in violation of the rules of the House, if the amendment had originated in the House, or an amendment by the Senate providing for an appropriation on a bill other than a general appropriation bill, may not be agreed to by the managers on the part of the House, unless specific authority to agree to such an amendment is first given by the House by a separate vote on each specific amendment.

MEETINGS AND ACTION OF CONFEREES

The meetings of the conferees are customarily held on the Senate side of the Capitol. In 1975, the House and the Senate adopted rules providing that conference meetings were to be open to the public except when the conferees of either the House or the Senate, in open session, determined by a roll call vote of a majority of those conferees present, that all or part of the meeting on the day of the vote would be closed to the public. However, in 1977, the House amended its rules to require that conference meetings be open, unless the House, in open session, determines by a roll call vote of a majority of those Members voting that all or part of the meeting will be closed to the public. When the report of the conference committee is read in the House, a point of order may be made that the conferees did not comply with this requirement. If the point of order is sustained, the conference report is considered rejected by the House and a new conference is requested.

There are generally four forms of recommendations available to the conferees when reporting back to their respective bodies:

(1) the Senate recede from all (or certain of) its amendments;
(2) the House recede from its disagreement to all (or certain of) the Senate amendments and agree thereto;
(3) the House recede from its disagreement to all (or certain of) the Senate amendments and agree thereto with amendments; and
(4) the House recede from all (or certain of) its amendments to the Senate amendments.

In many instances the result of the conference is a compromise growing out of the third type of recommendation available to the conferees. The complete report may, of course, be comprised of one, two, three, or all four of these recommendations with respect to the various amendments. Occasionally the conferees find themselves unable to reach an agreement with respect to one or more amendments and report back a statement of their inability to agree on those particular amendments. These may then be acted on separately. This partial disagreement is, of course, not practicable where the Senate strikes out all after the enacting clause and substitutes its own bill which must be considered as a single amendment.

If they are unable to reach any agreement whatsoever, the conferees report that fact to their respective bodies and the amendments are in the position they were before the conference was requested. New conferees may be appointed in either or both Houses. In addition, the Houses may instruct the conferees as to the position they are to take.

After House conferees on any bill or resolution in conference between the two bodies have been appointed for twenty calendar days and have failed to make a report, the House rules provide for a motion of the highest privilege to instruct the House conferees or discharge them and appoint new conferees. Further, during the last 6 days of a session, it is a privileged motion to move to discharge, appoint, or instruct House conferees after House conferees have been appointed 36 hours without having made a report.

CONFERENCE REPORTS

When the conferees, by majority vote of each group, have reached complete agreement (or find that they are able to agree with respect to some but not all amendments), they embody their recommendations in a report which must be signed by a majority of the conferees appointed by each body. The minority portion of the managers have no authority to file a statement of minority views in connection with the report. The report is required to be printed in both Houses and must be accompanied by an explanatory statement prepared jointly by the conferees on the part of the House and the conferees on the part of the Senate. (See Fig. 8. pp. 41 and 42.) The statement must be sufficiently detailed and explicit to inform the Congress as to the effect that the amendments or propositions contained in the report will have on the measure to which those amendments or propositions relate. The engrossed bill and amendments and one copy of the report are delivered to the body that is to act first on the report; namely, the body that had agreed to the conference requested by the other.

In the Senate, the presentation of the report is always in order except when the Journal is being read or a point of order or motion to adjourn is pending, or while the Senate is voting or ascertaining the presence of a quorum; and when received, the question of proceeding to the consideration of the report, if raised, is immediately voted on without debate. The report is not subject to amendment in either body and must be accepted or rejected as an entirety. If the time for debate on the adoption of the report is limited, the time allotted must be equally divided between the majority and minority party. If the Senate, acting first, does not agree to the report, it may by majority vote order it recommitted to the conferees. When the Senate agrees to the report its managers are thereby discharged and it then delivers the original papers to the House of Representatives with a message advising that body of its action.

The presentation of the report in the House of Representatives is always in order, except when the Journal is being read, while the roll is being called, or the House is dividing on any proposition. The report is considered in the House and may not be sent to the Committee of the Whole on the suggestion that it contains matters ordinarily requiring consideration in that Committee.

It is, however, not in order to consider either (1) a conference report or (2) an amendment (including an amendment in the nature of a substitute) proposed by the Senate to a measure reported in disagreement between the two Houses, until the third calendar day (excluding any Saturday, Sunday, or legal holiday) after the report and accompanying statement have been filed in the House, and consideration then is in order only if the report and accompanying statement have been printed in the daily edition of the *Congressional Record* for the day on which the report and statement have been filed; but these provisions do not apply during the last 6 days of the session. Nor is it in order to consider a conference report or such amendment unless copies of the report and accompanying statement, together with the text of the amendment, have been available to Members for at least two hours before the beginning of consideration; but it is always in order to call up for consideration a report from the Committee on Rules, making in order the consideration of a conference report or such amendment notwithstanding this restriction.

The time allotted for debate on a conference report or such amendment is equally divided between the majority party and the minority party. If the House does not agree to a conference report that the Senate has already agreed to, the report may not be recommitted to conference because the Senate conferees are discharged when the Senate agrees to the report.

When a conference report is called up before the House containing matter which would be in violation of the rules of the House with respect to germaneness if the matter had been offered as an amendment in the House, and which is contained either (1) in a Senate amendment to that measure (including a Senate amendment in the nature of a substitute for the text of that measure as passed by the House) and accepted by the House conferees or agreed to by the conference committee with modification or (2) in a substitute agreed to by the conference committee, it is in order, at any time after the reading of the statement, to make a point of order that nongermane matter, which must be specified in the point of order, is contained in the report. It is also in order to make a point of order to nongermane Senate matter in the conference report that originally appeared in the Senate bill but was not included in the House-passed version. If the point of order is sustained, it is then in order for the Chair to entertain a motion that the House reject the nongermane matter covered by the point of order.

Notwithstanding the final disposition of a point of order made with respect to the report, or of a motion to reject nongermane matter, further points of order may be made, and further motions may be made to reject other nongermane matter in the conference report not covered by any previous point of order which has been sustained. If a motion to reject has been adopted, after final disposition of all points of order and motions to reject, the conference report is considered as rejected and the question then pending before the House is whether (1) to recede and concur with an amendment that consists of that portion of the conference report not rejected or (2) to insist on the House amendment with respect to nongermane Senate matter that originally appeared in the Senate bill but was not included in the House-passed version. If all motions to reject are defeated, then, after the allocation of time for debate on the conference report equally divided between the majority and minority parties, it is in order to move the previous question on the adoption of the conference report.

CUSTODY OF PAPERS

The custody of the original official papers is important in conference procedure because either body may act only when in possession of the papers. As indicated above, the request for a conference may be made only by the body in possession. The papers are then transmitted to the body agreeing to the conference and by it to the managers of the House that asked. The latter in turn carry the papers with them to the conference and at its conclusion turn them over to the managers of the House that agreed to the conference. The managers deliver them to their own House, which acts first on the report, and then delivers the papers to the other House for final action.

Each group of conferees, at the conclusion of the conference, retains one copy of the report that has been made in duplicate, and signed by a majority of the managers of each body — the House copy signed first by the House managers and the Senate copy signed first by its managers.

Obviously a bill cannot become a law of the land until it has been approved in identical terms by both Houses of the Congress. When the bill has finally been approved by both Houses, all the original papers are transmitted to the enrolling clerk of the body in which the bill originated.

ENROLLMENT

When the bill has been agreed to in identical form by both bodies — either without amendment by the Senate, or by House concurrence in the Senate amendments, or by agreement in both bodies to the conference report — a copy of the bill is enrolled for presentation to the President.

The preparation of the enrolled bill is a painstaking though important task; it must reflect precisely the effect of all amendments, either by way of deletion, substitution, or addition, agreed to by both bodies. The enrolling clerk of the House (with respect to bills originating in the House) receives the original engrossed bill, the engrossed Senate amendments, the signed conference report, the several messages from the Senate, and a notation of the final action by the House, for the purpose of preparing the enrolled copy. From these he must prepare the final form of the bill, as it was agreed to by both Houses, for presentation to the President. On occasion there have been upward of 500 amendments, particularly after a conference, each of which must be set out in the enrollment exactly as agreed to, and all punctuation must be in accord with the action taken.

The enrolled bill is printed on parchment paper, with a certificate on the reverse side of the last page, to be signed by the Clerk of the House stating that the bill originated in the House of Representatives (or by the Secretary of the Senate when the bill has originated in that body). It is examined for accuracy by the Committee on House Administration (or by the Secretary of the Senate when the bill originated in that body). When the Committee is satisfied with the accuracy of the bill, the Chairman of the Committee attaches a slip stating that it finds the bill truly enrolled and sends it to the Speaker of the House for his signature. All bills, regardless of the body in which they originated, are signed first by the Speaker and then by the President of the Senate. The Speaker and the President of the Senate may sign bills only while their respective House is actually sitting unless advance permission is granted to sign during a recess or after adjournment. If the Speaker or the President of the Senate is unable to sign the bill, it may be signed by the authorized presiding officer of the respective House. After both signatures are affixed, the bill is ready for presentation to the President, as the Constitution so requires.

PRESIDENTIAL ACTION

The Constitution provides that—

Every Bill which shall have passed the House of Representatives and the Senate, shall, before it becomes a Law, be presented to the President of the United States.

In actual practice a clerk of the Committee on House Administration (or the Secretary of the Senate when the bill originated in that body) delivers the original enrolled bill to the White House and obtains a receipt. Delivery to the White House has customarily been regarded as presentation to the President and as commencing the 10-day Constitutional period for Presidential action.

Copies of the enrolled bill are usually transmitted by the White House to the various departments interested in the subject matter, so that they may advise the President who, of course, cannot be personally familiar with every item in every bill.

If the President approves the bill he signs it and usually writes the word "approved" and the date, the only Constitutional requirement being that he sign it. (See Fig. 9, p. 43 and 44.)

The bill may become law without the President's signature by virtue of the Constitutional provision that if he does not return a bill with his objections within 10 days (Sundays excepted) after it has been presented to him, it shall be a law in like manner as if he had signed it. (See Fig. 10, p. 45.) If, however, the Congress by their adjournment prevent its return, it does not become law. The latter event is what is known as a "pocket veto", that is, the bill does not become law even though the President has not sent his objections to the Congress.

Notice of the signing of a bill by the President is usually sent by message to the House in which it originated and that House informs the other, although this action is not necessary to the validity of the act. The action is also noted in the *Congressional Record*.

A bill becomes law on the date of approval (or passage over the President's veto), unless it expressly provides a different effective date.

VETO MESSAGE

By the terms of the Constitution, if the President does not approve the bill "he shall return it, with his objections to that House in which it shall have originated," — that is, veto it. It is the usual but not invariable rule that a bill returned with the President's objections, must be voted on at once and when laid before the House, the question on the passage is considered as pending. A vetoed bill is always privileged, and a motion to take it from the table is in order at any time.

The Member in charge moves the previous question which is put by the Speaker, as follows: "The question is, Will the House on reconsideration agree to pass the bill, the objections of the President to the contrary notwithstanding?" The Clerk calls the roll and those in favor of passing the bill answer "Aye", and those opposed "No". If fewer than two-thirds of the Members present (constituting a quorum) vote in the affirmative the bill is killed, and a message is usually sent to the Senate advising that body of the decision that the bill shall not pass. If, however, two-thirds vote in the affirmative, the bill is sent with the President's objections to the Senate, together with a message advising it of the action in the House.

There is a similar procedure in the Senate where again a two-thirds affirmative vote is necessary to pass the bill over the President's objections. If so passed by the Senate, the measure becomes the law of the land, notwithstanding the objections of the President, and it is ready for publication as a binding statute. (See Fig. 11, p. 46.)

The important process of the "publication" of a newly-enacted law will be examined in Part III below.

LEGISLATIVE VETO

At this point, we should mention the "legislative veto," a legislative technique intended to provide greater congressional control over executive branch actions. The legislative veto, also known as the "one-house veto" enables either the House or the Senate to unilaterally cancel certain executive branch actions. Congress has passed numerous laws which allow an executive agency to take certain actions — such as issuing regulations for federal elections — but which also allow the House and/or the Senate to cancel the actions with a one- or two-house veto.

The Congress "vetoes" (actually rescinds authority) by means of a concurrent or simple resolution. Concurrent or simple resolutions are used because neither must be sent to the President for his action. Congress could accomplish the same end by passing another bill to direct the President to take a desired action, but the President would then have an opportunity to veto. The original statute containing the "legislative veto" specifies whether action by one chamber (simple resolution) or both chambers (concurrent resolution) is necessary.

In January 1982, the U.S. Court of Appeals for the District of Columbia held that the congressional veto was unconstitutional. The decision, in a natural gas pricing case, could affect provisions in more than 200 federal statutes — ranging from foreign policy to the environment — which allow Congress to strike down executive actions on its own without further reference to the President.

The court said that legislative vetoes violate the fundamental allocation of power set out in the Constitution and allow Congress to intrude on executive authority. If Congress wants to tell the executive branch how to act or what to do, the court said, the Constitution provides only one way: by a vote of both houses of Congress which must then be sent to the President for his signature or veto. Supreme Court review of the issue is likely.

We will end the discussion here by a brief look at the *Congressional Record.* This will be immediately followed by a directory of selected Congressional telephone numbers and a list of selected Government publications on the subject of the legislative process.

Part II to follow below will discuss the budget process, which places special obligations on House and Senate committees in regard to spending and revenue proposals.

CONGRESSIONAL RECORD

At several points in our discussion, mention was made of the *Congressional Record.* The *Record,* printed daily when the Congress is in session, is a highly useful information source. It is available in most libraries or on a subscription basis through the Government Printing Office.

Floor debate in Congress on pending bills can occur at almost any stage of the legislative process, though typically it takes place after the bill has been reported out of committee. The *Congressional Record* provides a verbatim transcript (sometimes edited) of legislative debates and proceedings. Each daily issue contains an Appendix, or Extension of Remarks, which includes supplements to floor remarks, exhibits, such as newspaper editorials, and almost anything else a legislator wishes to insert.

Page sequence in the *Record* runs in three groups: S-number pages are the Senate record; H-number pages are the House record; and E-number pages are for Extension of Remarks (i.e., the Appendix referred to above).

A valuable part of the *Record* is the index, which is compiled every two weeks during the annual sessions of Congress and is cumulated after adjournment into one alphabetical index for the session. The index — maintained by subject, name of legislator, and title of legislation — covers items in both floor action and the Extension of Remarks. The index by legislator, for example, makes it possible to locate quickly the page references to every speech or passing remark made by any Member of Congress, every paper he introduced into the *Record,* and every piece of legislation he sponsored. (See Fig. 12, p. 47.) The index by subject (such as "social security" or "energy policy") enables you to learn who discussed the particular subject on the floor; what bills concerning it were introduced or acted upon by either House or by committees; and what articles or speeches relating to it were inserted into the *Record* in the Extension of Remarks.

Each daily issue of the *Record* also includes the "Daily Digest," which contains highlights of the session, summaries of proceedings, actions taken by both house, enactments signed by the President, and other useful information.

DIRECTORY INFORMATION
(See Also Inside Front Cover for Additional Telephone Listings)

HOUSE STANDING COMMITTEES

	Tel. No. (area code 202)		Tel. No. (area code 202)
Agriculture	225-2171	Judiciary	225-3951
Appropriations	225-2771	Merchant Marine and Fisheries	225-4047
Armed Services	225-4151	Post Office and Civil Service	225-4054
Banking, Finance and Urban Affairs	225-4247	Franking Commission	225-0436
Budget	225-7200	Public Works and Transportation	225-4472
District of Columbia	225-4457	Rules	225-9486
Education and Labor	225-4527	Minority	225-6991
Government Operations	225-5051	Science and Technology	225-6371
House Administration	225-2061	Small Business	225-5821
Interior and Insular Affairs	225-2761	Standards of Official Conduct	225-7103
International Relations	225-5021	Veterans' Affairs	225-3527
Interstate and Foreign Committee	225-2927	Ways and Means	225-3625

SENATE STANDING COMMITTEES

	Tel. No. (area code 202)		Tel. No. (area code 202)
Agriculture, Nutrition, and Forestry	224-2035	Governmental Affairs	224-4751
Appropriations	224-3471	Human Resources	224-5375
Armed Services	224-3871	Judiciary	224-5225
Banking, Housing and Urban Affairs	224-7391	Rules and Administration	224-6352
Budget	224-0642	Veterans' Affairs	224-9126
Commerce, Science & Transportation	224-5115	Select-Ethics	224-2981
Energy and Natural Resources	224-4971	Select-Indian Affairs	224-2251
Environment and Public Works	224-6176	Select-Intelligence	224-1700
Finance	224-4515	Select-Small Business	224-5175
Foreign Relations	224-4651	Special-Aging	224-5364

SELECT COMMITTEES

	Tel. No. (area code 202)		Tel. No. (area code 202)
Aging	225-9375	Narcotics Abuse and Control	225-1753
Congressional Operations	225-8267	Outer Continental Shelf	225-3426
Intelligence, Permanent	225-4121	Population	225-0542

JOINT COMMITTEES

	Tel. No. (area code 202)		Tel. No. (area code 202)
Economic	224-5171	Taxation	225-3621
Printing (Capitol)	224-5241		

MISCELLANEOUS CONGRESSIONAL NUMBERS

	Tel. No. (area code 202)		Tel. No. (area code 202)
Clerk of the House	225-7000	Joint Republican Leadership Office (Capitol)	225-6155
Bill Clerk	225-4470, 225-4421	Law Library	224-7558
Daily Digest	225-2868	Law Revision Counsel	225-3928
Library of House	225-0462	LEGIS Office (Bill Status)	225-1772
Library (Capitol)	225-2930	Legislative Counsel	225-6060
Congressional Black Caucus	225-1691	Legislative Reference	426-5700
Congressional Budget Office	225-1491	Library of House	225-0462
Congressional Directory	225-2240	Library (Capitol)	225-2930
Congressional Hispanic Caucus	225-2255	Library Station (Capitol)	225-3000
Congressional Record Index	224-1385	Majority Leader	225-8040
Congressional Research	426-5700	Majority Whip	225-5604
Congressional Rural Caucus	225-5080	Minority Clerk	225-8888
Democratic Caucus	225-9141	Minority Leader	225-0600
Democratic Congressional Committee	225-2758	Minority Whip	225-6201
Democratic Research Organization	225-8083	Parliamentarian	225-7373
Democratic Steering and Policy Committee	225-7187	Press Gallery	225-3945, 225-6772
Democratic Study Group	225-5858	Republican Congressional Committee	225-1800
Doorkeeper of House	225-3505	Republican Policy	225-6168
Publications Distribution Service	225-4355	Republican Research	225-0871
Guide Service (Capitol)	225-6827	Republican Study	225-0587
House Information Systems	225-9276	The Speaker's Office	225-5414
LEGIS Office (Bill Status)	225-1772	The Speaker's Rooms	225-2204
User Assistance Office	225-6002	The Speaker's Congressional Office	225-5111

SELECT LIST OF GOVERNMENT PUBLICATIONS*

How Our Laws Are Made, Revised and Updated by Edward F. Willett, Jr., Esq., Law Revision Counsel, U.S. House Representatives: House Document No. 96-352, 96th Congress, 2d Session, 1980. The material in Part I above was extracted in part from this publication.

Senate Legislative Procedural Flow (and related House action), prepared by Harold G. Ast, Legislative Clerk, under direction of J. Stanley Kimmitt, Secretary of the Senate, November, 1978.

Constitution of the United States of America, Analysis and Interpretation, with annotations of cases decided by the Supreme Court of the United States to June 29, 1972; prepared by the Congressional Research Service, Library of Congress, Johnny H. Killian, editor, and Lester S. Jayson, supervising editor. Supplements published periodically.

House Rules and Manual:
   Constitution, Jefferson's Manual, and Rules of the House of Representatives of the United States, prepared by Wm. Holmes Brown, Parliamentarian of the House. New editions are published each Congress.

Senate Manual:
   Containing the standing rules, orders, laws, and resolutions affecting the business of the United States Senate; Jefferson's Manual, Declaration of Independence, Articles of Confederation, Constitution of the United States, etc. Prepared under the direction of the Senate Committee on Rules and Administration. New editions are published each Congress.

Hinds' Precedents of the House of Representatives:
   Including references to provisions of the Constitution, laws, and decisions of the Senate, by Asher C. Hinds.
      Vols. 1-5 (1907).
      Vols. 6-8 (1935), as compiled by Clarence Cannon, are supplementary to vols. 1-5 and cover the 28-year period from 1907 to 1935, revised up to and including the 73d Congress.
      Vols. 9-11 (1941) are index-digest to vols. 1-5.

Deschler's Precedents of the United States House of Representatives:
   Including references to provisions of the Constitution and laws, and to decisions of the courts, covering the period from 1936 to 1974, by Lewis Deschler, J.D., D.J., M.P.L., LL.D., Parliamentarian of the House (1928-1974).
      Vols. 1-3 have been published, additional volumes in preparation.

Cannon's Procedure in the House of Representatives:
   By Clarence Cannon, A.M., LL.B., LL.D., Member of Congress, sometime Parliamentarian of the House, Speaker pro tempore, Chairman of the Committee of the Whole, Chairman of Committee on Appropriations, etc.

Deschler's Procedure in the U.S. House of Representatives, Third Edition (1978):
   By Lewis Deschler, J.D., D.J., M.P.L., LL.D., Parliamentarian of the House (1928-1974), and Wm. Holmes Brown, Parliamentarian of the House (1974—).

Senate Procedure:
   By Floyd M. Riddick, Parliamentarian of the Senate: Senate Document No. 93-21 (1974).

Digest of Public General Bills and Resolutions:
   A brief synopsis of public bills and resolutions, and changes made therein during the legislative process; prepared by American Law Division, Congressional Research Service, Library of Congress, and published during each session in 5 or more cumulative issues with biweekly supplementation as needed.

Congressional Record:
   Proceedings and debates of the House and Senate, published daily, and bound with an index and history of bills and resolutions at the conclusion of each session of the Congress.

United States Statutes at Large:
   Containing the laws and concurrent resolutions enacted, and reorganization plans and proclamations promulgated during each session of the Congress, published annually under the direction of the Administrator of General Services by the Office of the Federal Register, National Archives and Records Service, General Services Administration, Washington, D.C. 20408.

United States Treaties and Other International Agreements:
   Compiled and published annually since 1950 under the direction of the Secretary of State.

Treaties and Other International Agreements of the United States of America, 1776-1949:
   A consolidation of the texts of treaties and other international agreements prior to 1950, compiled under the direction of Charles I. Bevans, Assistant Legal Adviser, Department of State, volumes I-XII (index volume in preparation).

United States Code:
   The general and permanent laws of the United States in force on the day preceding the commencement of the session following the last session the legislation of which is included; arranged in 50 titles; prepared under the direction and supervision of the Law Revision Counsel of the House of Representatives. New editions are published every 6 years and cumulative supplements are published annually.

Federal Register:
   Presidential Proclamations, Executive Orders, and Federal agency orders, regulations, and notices, and general documents of public applicability and legal effect, published daily. The regulations therein amend the Code of Federal Regulations. Published by the Office of the Federal Register, National Archives and Records Service, General Service Administration, Washington, D.C. 20408.

---

*For sale by the Superintendent of Documents, U.S. Government Printing Office, Washington, D.C. 20402.

Code of Federal Regulations:

Cumulates in bound volumes the general and permanent rules and regulations of Federal agencies published in the Federal Register, including Presidential documents. Each volume of the Code is revised at least once each calendar year and issued on a quarterly basis. Published by the Office of the Federal Register, National Archives and Records Service, General Services Administration, Washington, D.C. 20408.

Weekly Compilation of Presidential Documents:

Containing statements, messages, and other Presidential materials released by the White House up to 5:00 p.m. Friday of each week, published every Monday by the Office of the Federal Register, National Archives and Records Service, General Services Administration, Washington, D.C. 20408.

Public papers of the Presidents of the United States:

Containing public messages and statements, verbatim transcript of the President's News Conference and other selected papers released by the White House each year, since 1945, compiled by the Office of the Federal Register, National Archives and Records Service, General Services Administration, Washington, D.C. 20408.

Figure 1 — Introduced Bill*

94TH CONGRESS
1ST SESSION

H. R. 5727

IN THE HOUSE OF REPRESENTATIVES

APRIL 8, 1975

Mr. KASTENMEIER (for himself, Mr. RODINO, Mr. RAILSBACK, Mr. DANIELSON, Mr. DRINAN, Mr. BADILLO, Mr. PATTISON of New York, Mr. WIGGINS, Mr. EDWARDS of California, Mr. CONYERS, Mr. ELIBERG, Mr. SEIBERLING, Ms. HOLTZMAN, Mr. MEZVINSKY, and Mr. COHEN) introduced the following bill; which was referred to the Committee on the Judiciary

---

A BILL

To establish an independent and regionalized United States Parole Commission, to provide fair and equitable parole procedures, and for other purposes.

1   *Be it enacted by the Senate and House of Representa-*

2   *tives of the United States of America in Congress assembled,*

3   That this Act may be cited as the "Parole Reorganization

4   Act of 1975".

    *   *   *   *   *   *   *

(Sample copy of part of first page and end of last page of this 33-page introduced bill)

    *   *   *   *   *   *   *

7   EFFECTIVE DATE

8   SEC. 3. This Act shall take effect sixty days after the

9   date of enactment.

---

*All illustrations in this document are reduced in size.

Figure 2 — Reported Print

Union Calendar No. 80

94TH CONGRESS
1ST SESSION

H. R. 5727

[Report No. 94–184]

IN THE HOUSE OF REPRESENTATIVES

APRIL 8, 1975

Mr. KASTENMEIER (for himself, Mr. RODINO, Mr. RAILSBACK, Mr. DANIELSON, Mr. DRINAN, Mr. BADILLO, Mr. PATTISON of New York, Mr. WIGGINS, Mr. EDWARDS of California, Mr. CONYERS, Mr. ELIBERG, Mr. SEIBERLING, Ms. HOLTZMAN, Mr. MEZVINSKY, and Mr. COHEN) introduced the following bill; which was referred to the Committee on the Judiciary

MAY 1, 1975

Reported with amendments, committed to the Committee of the Whole House on the State of the Union, and ordered to be printed

[Omit the part struck through and insert the part printed in italic]

A BILL

To establish an independent and regionalized United States Parole Commission, to provide fair and equitable parole procedures, and for other purposes.

1   *Be it enacted by the Senate and House of Representa-*

2   *tives of the United States of America in Congress assembled,*

3   *That this Act may be cited as the "Parole Reorganization*

4   *Act of 1975".*

*   *   *   *   *   *   *

(Sample copy of part of first page and end of last page of this 33-page reported bill)

*   *   *   *   *   *   *

7   EFFECTIVE DATE

8   SEC. 3. This Act shall take effect sixty days after the

9   date of enactment.

Figure 3 — House Committee Report*

94TH CONGRESS } HOUSE OF REPRESENTATIVES { REPORT
1st Session } { No. 94–184

PAROLE REORGANIZATION ACT OF 1975

MAY 1, 1975.—Committed to the Committee of the Whole House on the State of
the Union and ordered to be printed

Mr. KASTENMEIER, from the Committee on the Judiciary,
submitted the following

REPORT

[To accompany H.R. 5727]

The Committee on the Judiciary, to whom was referred the bill
(H.R. 5727) to amend title 18 of the United States Code to reorganize
the United States Board of Parole, having considered the same, report
favorably thereon with amendments and recommend that the bill as
amended do pass.

The amendments are as follows:

1. On page 19, line 9, strike "§ 2410" and insert in lieu thereof
"§ 4210,"

2. On page 27, line 7, strike "4213(c)" and insert in lieu thereof
"4213(a)".

PURPOSE OF THE AMENDMENTS

The amendments are corrections of typographical errors.

PURPOSE OF THE AMENDED BILL

H.R. 5727 deals with two major questions:

1. It would reconstitute the U.S. Parole Board as the U.S. Parole
Commission, an independent agency within the Department of Justice,
organized into five geographic regions with definite statutory powers
and obligations.

2. It would provide an infusion of procedural protections into the
Federal parole system at the initial determination stage as well as the
appellate and revocation levels. The purpose of these changes is to insure a fair and equitable parole process.

BACKGROUND

The Parole Reorganization Act of 1975 is the work product of hun-
dreds of hours of effort by the House Judiciary Committee including:
21 days of public hearings by the Subcommittee on Courts, Civil Lib-

*First page only.

Figure 4 — Engrossed Bill*

94TH CONGRESS
1ST SESSION
H. R. 5727

AN ACT

To establish an independent and regionalized United States Parole Commission, to provide fair and equitable parole procedures, and for other purposes.

1   *Be it enacted by the Senate and House of Representa-*

2   *tives of the United States of America in Congress assembled,*

3   That this Act may be cited as the "Parole Reorganization

4   Act of 1975".

*   *   *   *   *   *   *

(Sample copy of part of first page and end of last page of this 33-page engrossed bill)

*   *   *   *   *   *   *

7   EFFECTIVE DATE

8   SEC. 3. This Act shall take effect sixty days after the

9   date of enactment.

Passed the House of Representatives May 21, 1975.

Attest: W. PAT JENNINGS,

Clerk.

---

*Printed on blue paper.

Figure 5 — Senate Referred ("Act") Print

94TH CONGRESS
1ST SESSION

H. R. 5727

IN THE SENATE OF THE UNITED STATES

MAY 22, 1975

Read twice and referred to the Committee on the Judiciary

AN ACT

To establish an independent and regionalized United States Parole Commission, to provide fair and equitable parole procedures, and for other purposes.

1   *Be it enacted by the Senate and House of Representa-*

2 *tives of the United States of America in Congress assembled,*

3 That this Act may be cited as the "Parole Reorganization

4 Act of 1975".

    *   *   *   *   *   *   *

(Sample copy of part of first page and end of last page of this 33-page bill as passed by House and referred to committee in Senate)

    *   *   *   *   *   *   *

7   EFFECTIVE DATE

8   SEC. 3. This Act shall take effect sixty days after the

9 date of enactment.

Passed the House of Representatives May 21, 1975.

Attest: W. PAT JENNINGS,

Clerk.

Figure 6 — Senate Reported Print

Calendar No. 362

94TH CONGRESS
1ST SESSION
H. R. 5727

[Report No. 94–369]

IN THE SENATE OF THE UNITED STATES

MAY 22, 1975

Read twice and referred to the Committee on the Judiciary

SEPTEMBER 11, 1975

Reported by Mr. BURDICK, with amendments

[Strike out all after the enacting clause and insert the part printed in italic]

AN ACT

To establish an independent and regionalized United States Parole Commission, to provide fair and equitable parole procedures, and for other purposes.

1   *Be it enacted by the Senate and House of Representa-*

2   *tives of the United States of America in Congress assembled,*

3   ~~That this Act may be cited as the "Parole Reorganization~~

4   ~~Act of 1975".~~

        *   *   *   *   *   *   *

(Sample copy of part of first page and end of last page of this 63-page bill as reported to Senate for its consideration)

        *   *   *   *   *   *   *

2   *Commission may make such transitional rules as are neces-*

3   *sary to be in effect for not to exceed one year following such*

4   *effective date.*

        Amend the title so as to read: "An Act to amend title 18, United States Code, relating to parole, and for other purposes."

        Passed the House of Representatives May 21, 1975.

        Attest: W. PAT JENNINGS,

                                                    Clerk.

Figure 7 — Senate Committee Report*

Calendar No. 362

94TH CONGRESS 1st Session	SENATE	REPORT No. 94-369

THE PAROLE COMMISSION ACT

SEPTEMBER 11, 1975.—Ordered to be printed

Mr. BURDICK, from the Committee on the Judiciary, submitted the
following

REPORT

[To accompany H.R. 5727]

The Committee on the Judiciary, to which was referred (H.R. 5727)
an act to establish an independent and regional United States Parole
Commission, to provide fair and equitable aprole procedures, and for
other purposes, having considered the same, reports favorably thereon
with an amendment in the nature of a substitute, and recommends that
the bill as amended do pass.

AMENDMENT

The Committee made the following amendment to the bill as
originally introduced:
Strike out all after the enacting clause and insert in lieu thereof
the following:
That this Act may be cited as the "Parole Commission Act".
SEC. 2. Chapter 311 of title 18, United States Code, is amended to
read as follows:

"CHAPTER 311—PAROLE

"Sec.
"4201. Definitions.
"4202. Parole Commission created.
"4203. Powers and duties of the Commission.
"4204. Powers and duties of the Chairman.
"4205. Persons eligible.
"4206. Release on parole.
"4207. Conditions of parole.
"4208. Parole interviews procedures.
"4209. Aliens.
"4210. Retaking parole violator under warrant.
"4211. Officer executing warrant to retake parole violator.
"4212. Parole modification and revocation.
"4213. Reconsideration and appeal.
"4214. Original jurisdiction cases.
"4215. Applicability of Administrative Procedure Act.
"4216. Young adult offenders.
"4217. Warrants to retake Canal Zone violators.

*First page only.

Figure 8 — Conference Committee Report

94TH CONGRESS 2d Session	HOUSE OF REPRESENTATIVES	REPORT No. 94–838

PAROLE COMMISSION AND REORGANIZATION ACT

FEBRUARY 23, 1976.—Ordered to be printed

Mr. KASTENMEIER, from the committee of conference, submitted the following

CONFERENCE REPORT

[To accompany H.R. 5727]

The committee of conference on the disagreeing votes of the two Houses on the amendment of the Senate to the bill (H.R. 5727) to establish an independent and regionalized United States Parole Commission, to provide fair and equitable parole procedures, and for other purposes, having met, after full and free conference, have agreed to recommend and do recommend to their respective Houses as follows:

In lieu of the matter proposed to be inserted by the Senate amendment insert the following:

That this Act may be cited as the "Parole Commission and Reorganization Act."

UNITED STATES PAROLE COMMISSION; PAROLE PROCEDURES, CONDITIONS, ETC.

SECTION 2. Title 18 of the United States Code is amended by repealing chapter 311 (relating to parole) and inserting in lieu thereof the following new chapter to read as follows:

*   *   *   *   *   *   *

(Sample copy of part of first page and end of page 17 of conference report)

*   *   *   *   *   *   *

And the Senate agree to the same.

> ROBERT W. KASTENMEIER,
> GEORGE DANIELSON,
> ROBERT F. DRINAN,
> HERMAN BADILLO,
> EDWARD W. PATTISON,
> TOM RAILSBACK,
> CHARLES E. WIGGINS,
> *Managers on the Part of the House.*
> QUENTIN N. BURDICK,
> ROMAN L. HRUSKA,
> JOHN L. McCLELLAN,
> CHARLES McC. MATHIAS, Jr.,
> EDWARD KENNEDY,
> *Managers on the Part of the Senate.*

Figure 8 — Continued

JOINT EXPLANATORY STATEMENT OF THE COMMITTEE OF CONFERENCE

The managers on the part of the House and Senate at the conference on the disagreeing votes of the two Houses on the amendment of the Senate to the bill (H.R. 5727) to establish an independent and regionalized United States Parole Commission, to provide fair and equitable parole procedures, and for other purposes, submit the following joint statement to the House and the Senate in explanation of the effect of the action agreed upon by the managers and recommend in the accompanying conference report:

*   *   *   *   *   *   *

(Sample copy of part of page 19 and end of last page of this 37-page conference report)

*   *   *   *   *   *   *

SEC. 15. This section authorizes the appropriation of such sums as are necessary to carry out the purposes of this Act.

SEC. 16. (a) This subsection transfers personnel, liabilities, etc., of the U.S. Board of Parole to the Chairman of the U.S. Parole Commission.

(b) This legislation takes effect 60 days after enactment, except that the provisions of section 4208(h) shall take effect 120 days after enactment.

(c) All members of the U.S. Board of Parole on the effective date of this legislation would become commissioners entitled to serve for the remainder of the terms for which they were appointed as members of the U.S. Board of Parole.

(d) The purpose of this section is to insure that service as a member of the United States Board of Parole prior to the effective date of this Act shall not be counted toward the twelve-year limitation on terms of U.S. Parole Commissioners provided by this Act. It is the intent of the Conferees that this provision be liberally construed so that a person who has two years of his term as a U.S. Parole Commissioner, be eligible for reappointment for a six-year term as a member of the U.S. Parole Commission and be eligible again for reappointment for whatever period of time would be necessary so that he would be entitled to twelve years of service as a U.S. Parole Commissioner.

ROBERT W. KASTENMEIER,
GEORGE DANIELSON,
ROBERT F. DRINAN,
HERMAN BADILLO,
EDWARD W. PATTISON,
TOM RAILSBACK,
CHARLES E. WIGGINS,
Managers on the Part of the House.
QUENTIN N. BURDICK,
ROMAN L. HRUSKA,
JOHN L. MCCLELLAN,
CHARLES McC. MATHIAS, Jr.,
EDWARD KENNEDY,
Managers on the Part of the Senate.

Figure 9 — Enrolled Bill Signed by President

H. R. 5727   PUBLIC LAW 94-233

Ninety-fourth Congress of the United States of America

AT THE SECOND SESSION

*Begun and held at the City of Washington on Monday, the nineteenth day of January,
one thousand nine hundred and seventy-six*

An Act

To establish an independent and regionalized United States Parole Commission,
to provide fair and equitable parole procedures, and for other purposes.

*Be it enacted by the Senate and House of Representatives of the
United States of America in Congress assembled,* That this Act may
be cited as the "Parole Commission and Reorganization Act".

UNITED STATES PAROLE COMMISSION ; PAROLE PROCEDURES, CONDITIONS, ETC.

SEC. 2. Title 18 of the United States Code is amended by repealing
chapter 311 (relating to parole) and inserting in lieu thereof the
following new chapter to read as follows:

"Chapter 311—PAROLE

"Sec.
"4201. Definitions.
"4202. Parole Commission created.
"4203. Powers and duties of the Commission.
"4204. Powers and duties of the Chairman.
"4205. Time of eligibility for release on parole.
"4206. Parole determination criteria.
"4207. Information considered.
"4208. Parole determination proceeding ; time.
"4209. Conditions of parole.
"4210. Jurisdiction of Commission.
"4211. Early termination of parole.
"4212. Aliens.
"4213. Summons to appear or warrant for retaking of parolee.
"4214. Revocation of parole.
"4215. Reconsideration and appeal.
"4216. Young adult offenders.
"4217. Warrants to retake Canal Zone parole violators.
"4218. Applicability of Administrative Procedure Act.

"§ 4201. Definitions

"As used in this chapter—
"(1) 'Commission' means the United States Parole Commission;
"(2) 'Commissioner' means any member of the United States
Parole Commission;
"(3) 'Director' means the Director of the Bureau of Prisons;
"(4) 'Eligible prisoner' means any Federal prisoner who is
eligible for parole pursuant to this title or any other law including
any Federal prisoner whose parole has been revoked and who
is not otherwise ineligible for parole;
"(5) 'Parolee' means any eligible prisoner who has been released
on parole or deemed as if released on parole under section 4164 or
section 4205(f) ; and
"(6) 'Rules and regulations' means rules and regulations promulgated by the Commission pursuant to section 4203 and section
553 of title 5, United States Code.

"§ 4202. Parole Commission created

"There is hereby established, as an independent agency in the
Department of Justice, a United States Parole Commission which shall

Figure 9 — Continued

H. R. 5727—15

Sec. 11. Section 5041 of title 18, United States Code, is amended to read as follows:

"§ 5041. Parole

"A juvenile delinquent who has been committed may be released on parole at any time under such conditions and regulations as the United State Parole Commission deems proper in accordance with the provisions in section 4206 of this title."

Sec. 12. Whenever in any of the laws of the United States or the District of Columbia the term "United States Parole Board", or any other term referring thereto, is used, such term or terms, on and after the date of the effective date of this Act, shall be deemed to refer to the United States Parole Commission as established by the amendments made by this Act.

Sec. 13. Section 5108(c)(7) of title 5, United States Code, is amended to read as follows:

"(7) the Attorney General, without regard to any other provision of this section, may place a total of ten positions of warden in the Bureau of Prisons in GS–16;".

Sec. 14. Section 3655 of title 18, United States Code, relating to duties of probation officers, is amended by striking out "Attorney General" in the last sentence and inserting in lieu thereof "United States Parole Commission".

Sec. 15. There is hereby authorized to be appropriated such sums as are necessary to carry out the purposes of the amendments made by this Act.

Sec. 16. (a) There are hereby transferred to the Chairman of the United States Parole Commission, all personnel, liabilities, contracts, property and records as are employed, held, used, arising from, available or to be made available of the United States Board of Parole with respect to all functions, powers, and duties transferred by this Act to the United States Parole Commission.

(b) This Act shall take effect sixty days after the date of enactment, except that the provisions of section 4208(h) of this Act shall take effect one hundred twenty days after the date of enactment.

(c) Each person holding office as a member of the United States Board of Parole on the day before the effective date of the Parole Commission and Reorganization Act shall be a Commissioner whose term as such shall expire on the date of the expiration of the term for which such person was appointed as a member of the Board of Parole.

(d) For the purpose of section 4202 of title 18, United States Code, service by an individual as a member of the United States Board of Parole shall not constitute service as a Commissioner.

Speaker of the House of Representatives.

President of the Senate pro tempore.

APPROVED

MAR 15 1976

**Figure 10 — Copy of Act which became a law
without approval of the President**

Public Law 94-4
94th Congress, H. R. 1589
February 20, 1975

An Act

To suspend increases in the costs of coupons to food stamp recipients as a result
of recent administrative actions.

*Be it enacted by the Senate and House of Representatives of the
United States of America in Congress assembled,* That, notwithstanding the provisions of section 7(b) of the Food Stamp Act of
1964 (7 U.S.C. 2016(b)), the charge imposed on any household for a
coupon allotment under such Act after the date of enactment of this
Act and prior to December 30, 1975, may not exceed the charge that
would have been imposed on such household for such coupon allotment
under rules and regulations promulgated under such Act and in effect
on January 1, 1975.

Food stamp
coupons.
Cost increase,
suspension.
7 USC 2016
note.

[Note by the Office of the Federal Register.—The foregoing Act, having
been presented to the President of the United States on Friday, February 7,
1975, for his approval and not having been returned by him to the House of
Congress in which it originated within the time prescribed by the Constitution
of the United States, has become a law without his approval on February 20,
1975.]

LEGISLATIVE HISTORY:

HOUSE REPORT No. 94-2 (Comm. on Agriculture).
CONGRESSIONAL RECORD, Vol. 121 (1975):
    Feb. 4, considered and passed House.
    Feb. 5, considered and passed Senate, in lieu of S. 35.
WEEKLY COMPILATION OF PRESIDENTIAL DOCUMENTS, Vol. 11, No. 7:
    Feb. 13, Presidential statement.

Figure 11 — Endorsements on Act which became a law after Presidential veto

Public Law 96–264
June 6, 1980
96th Congress, H.R. 7428

THOMAS P. O'NEILL, JR.
Speaker of the House of Representatives.

WARREN G. MAGNUSON
President of the Senate pro Tempore.

IN THE HOUSE OF REPRESENTATIVES, U.S.,
June 5, 1980.

The House of Representatives having proceeded to reconsider the bill (H.R. 7428) entitled "An Act to extend the present public debt limit through June 30, 1980", returned by the President of the United States with his objections, to the House of Representatives, in which it originated, it was

Resolved, That the said bill pass, two-thirds of the House of Representatives agreeing to pass the same.

EDMUND L. HENSHAW, JR.
Clerk.

By Thomas E. Ladd
Assistant to the Clerk.

I certify that this Act originated in the House of Representatives.

EDMUND L. HENSHAW, JR.
Clerk.

By Thomas E. Ladd
Assistant to the Clerk.

IN THE SENATE OF THE UNITED STATES,
June 6 (legislative day, January 3), 1980.

The Senate having proceeded to reconsider the bill (H.R. 7428) entitled "An Act to extend the present public debt limit through June 30, 1980", returned by the President of the United States with his objections, to the House of Representatives, in which it originated, and passed by the House of Representatives on reconsideration of the same, it was

Resolved, That the said bill pass, two-thirds of the Senators present having voted in the affirmative.

Attest:

J. S. KIMMITT
Secretary.

Figure 12 — Congressional Record Index

Moynihan, Daniel Patrick

Remarks by, on
Adoption: national computerized identification center (S. 989), S3867•
AFDC: assessment of welfare program, S3227•
———functional alternatives to work requirements for recipients (S. 986), S3859•
———gradual Federal takeover of local share (S. 853), S3210•
———matching formula for States which meet certain requirements (S. 855), S3214•
Artistic compositions: tax deduction for contribution to charities (S. 851, 852), S3208•, S3209
AWACS aircraft: Saudi Arabia request, S3921•
Budget: debate procedure for S. Con. Res. 9, S2982, S2983
———education, S2982, S2983, S2986, S2993–S2995
———reconciliation revision for 1981–83 (S. Con. Res. 9), S2935•, S2982, S2983, S2986, S2990, S2993–S2996, S3125, S3132–S3134, S3149, S3151, S3179, S3181, S3273, S3274, S3278–S3280, S3282, S3284, S3287, S3305•, S3315
———social programs, S3227•
Cities: urban development action grant program, S3305•
Coalition for a Democratic Majority: UN Ambassador Kirkpatrick honored, S2968
Education: Pell grants and student loans, S2982, S2983, S2986, S2993–S2995
Expatriates' Tax Act: U.S. citizens living/working abroad (S. 867), S3373•
F-15 aircraft: enhanced equipment requested by Saudi Arabia, S3921•
Federal Deposit Insurance Corp.: variable-rate debentures (S. 985), S3857•
Federal Savings and Loan Insurance Corp.: variable-rate debentures (S. 985), S3857•
Federal spending: regional imbalance, S3278–S3280
Foreign relations: bipartisanship, S2968
Handgun Crime Control Act (S. 974), S3814•
Kirkpatrick, Jeane: bipartisanship in foreign policy, S2968
Legal Services Corp.: funds, S3179
Mass transit: funds, S3273, S3274
Medicaid: administration proposal, S
———impact on State budget and F bility, S3210•
———matching formula for States tain requirements (S. 855), S3214•
———Puerto Rico, S3282, S3287
New York, N.Y.: mass transit funds, S3273, S3274
PLO: U.S. contribution and controversial organizations, S3225, S3751
Puerto Rico: medicaid, S3282, S3287
Reader's Digest: death of Dewitt Wallace, S3401•
Reagan, President: assassination attempt, S2982
———medical report, S3288
Saudi Arabia: sale of AWACS aircraft, S3921•
Social programs: administration budget request, S3227•
Social security: minimum benefits, S2935•
Taxation: artistic compositions contributed to charities (S. 851, 852), S3208•, S3209
———deductions, credits and exemptions, S3149
———U.S. citizens living/working abroad (S. 867), S3373•
UN: Ambassador Jeane Kirkpatrick, S2968
———U.S. contribution and PLO-related organizations, S3225, S3751
Wallace, Dewitt: eulogy, S3401•
Wallenberg, Raoul: honorary U.S. citizenship (S.J. Res. 65), S3604
———1944 disappearance of Swedish diplomat, S3604
Welfare: AFDC program, S3227•
———gradual Federal takeover of local share of AFDC and medicaid (S. 853), S3210•
———program to test the ability of State to develop fundamental alternatives to AFDC work requirements (S. 986), S3859•
Women: equality of economic opportunities (S. 888), S3527•
Work Incentive Demonstration Program Act(S. 986), S3859•

Youth: training programs, S3125
Statement
Surface Transportation Act, by, S3274
Tables
Federal spending, by State, S3279
Mass transit expenses covered by Federal aid, by city, S3274
MULLER, STEVEN
Letter
Student aid program proposed budget reductions, Johns Hopkins University, H1301
MUNICIPALITIES see URBAN AREAS.
MUNROE, GEORGE B.
Address
Environmental Suffocation, E1673
MURCHISON, WILLIAM
Articles and editorials
Lefever Outrages Left With Human Rights Views, S3606
MURKOWSKI, FRANK H. *(a Senator from Alaska)*
Appointment
Acting President pro tempore, S3767
Articles and editorials
Double Whammy, Anchorage (Alaska) Times, S3229•
Bills and resolutions introduced by
Blinded Veterans Recognition Day: designate (see S.J. Res. 64), S3684
POW/MIA Recognition Day: designate (see S.J. Res. 50), S3747
Presidential assassination attempt: tribute to security officers (see S. Res. 106), S3266, S3267
Yukon River barge service: sale to city of Nenana, Alaska (see S. 870), S3346
Remarks by, on
Budget: reconciliation revision for 1981–83 (S. Con. Res, 9), S2941, S2947, S2980, S3035
Economic Development Administration: funds, S3035
Jenes, Theodore: transfer, S3228•

Bills and resolutions introduced by
African Refugee Relief Day: designate (see H.J. Res. 202), H1218
Aliens: social security card procedures (see H.R. 2490), H1484
Butka, Kap S.: relief (see H.R. 3013), H1296
Charities: increase tax deduction allowable for property to be used for education, research, or experimentation (see H.R. 2472), H1428
Deaf: provide for teletypewriters in the House of Representatives (see H. Res. 125), H1392
Deaf or speech-impaired persons: tax credit for use of toll telephone service by means of teletypewriters (see H.R. 3070), H1390
Export Trading Act: enact (see H.R. 1799), H1484
Exports: establish national policy (see H.R. 3173), H1460
Foreign trade: enact Export Trading Act (see H.R. 1799), H1484
Gas and electricity master meters: prohibit certain use (see H.R. 1686), H1392
Gluzman, Semyon, and family: implore Soviet Union to allow to emigrate to Israel (see H.J. Res. 230), H1461
Grain: establish national insurance program to protect persons storing, in public warehouse (see H.R. 2523), H1393
Highway bridges: increase Federal share payable for replacement and rehabilitation projects (see H.R. 3227), H1483
House of Representatives: provide for centrally located teletypewriter facilities (see H. Res. 125), H1392
Individual retirement accounts: tax deduction for certain persons (see H.R. 2617), H1428

Individuals and businesses: tax reform and tax incentives (see H.R. 3050), H1389
Insurance: prohibit discrimination (see H.R. 100), H1297
Married individuals: tax rate (see H.R. 2474), H1428
Oil: exemption from crude oil windfall profit tax for independent producers and royalty owners (see H.R. 2451), H1462
———facilitate production from tar sand and other hydrocarbon deposits (see H.R. 3114), H1391
Pearl Harbor Survivors Association: incorporate (see H.R. 2022), H1428
Poland: call upon Soviet Union not to intervene in domestic affairs of (see H. Con. Res. 91), H1393
Programs and Papers Portraying the Personality, Character, and Achievements of George Washington: print (see H. Res. 79), H1393
Social security: card procedures (see H.R. 2490), H1484
———flexible income contribution and resource standards for couples in which one spouse is in a nursing home (see H.R. 2615), H1248
Soviet Union: call upon not to intervene in domestic affairs of Poland (see H. Con. Res. 91), H1393
———implore to allow Dr. Semyon Gluzman, and family to emigrate to Israel (see H.J. Res. 230), H1461
Speech-impaired persons: provide for teletypewriters in the House of Representatives (see H. Res. 125), H1392
Taxation: credit for deaf or speech-impaired persons for use of toll telephone service by means of teletypewriters (see H.R. 3070), H1390
———deduction for individual retirement savings for certain persons (see H.R. 2617), H1428
———increase charitable contribution deduction allowable for property to be used for education, research, or experimentation (see H.R. 2472), H1428
———married·individuals (see H.R. 2474), H1428
———reform and incentives for individuals and e H.R. 3050), H1389
: tax credit for deaf or speech-im- s for use of (see H.R. 3070), H1390
award special gold medal to (see), H1275
eorge: mint half dollars with design of 250th anniversary of birth (see H.R. 2524), H1428
Letter
Review and report on our policies regarding foreign control of U.S. minerals, by, E1809
List
H.R. 1776, honor roll, E1796
Remarks by, on
Atlanta, Ga.: Federal aid to help solve murders of black children (H. Con. Res. 99), E1562•
Blacks: Federal help in solving murders of children in Atlanta, Ga. (H. Con. Res. 99), E1562•
Children: Federal help in Atlanta, Ga. murders (H. Con. Res. 99), E1562•
International Year of Disabled Persons: observance (H. Con. Res. 55), E1798•
MURTHA, JOHN P. *(a Representative from Pennsylvania)*
Address
Role of Scouting in Helping to Promote the Role of Women in Today's Society, Donald H. Trautlein, E1584•
Articles and editorials
Vietnam's Gulag Is Too Familiar To Absorb, William F. Buckley, Jr., E1589•
Bills and resolutions introduced by
African Refugee Relief Day: designate (see H.J. Res. 202), H1218
Waring, Fred: award special gold medal to (see H.J. Res. 223), H1275
Remarks by, on
Burton, Homer M.: tribute, E1581•
Du Pont, B. T.: tribute, E1581•
Holloway, Perry: tribute, E1581•
Johnstown, Pa.: tribute to Talus Rock Girl Scout Council, E1584•

SAMPLE PAGE FROM CONGRESSIONAL RECORD INDEX

PART II
THE BUDGET PROCESS

The Congressional budget process is closely related to the process through which legislative proposals in general are enacted into law, the basic stages of which were discussed in Part I. Proposals for the spending of federal monies, generally, like other Congressional bills, must work their way through the legislative process if they are to become law.

Spending proposals are referred to House and Senate Appropriations Committees, who in turn refer the detailed work to subcommittees. These subcommittees have jurisdiction over specific departments and agencies (i.e., the Defense subcommittee, the Labor/HHS subcommittee, the HUD subcommittee, etc.).

The Congressional "reconciliation" procedure is an important exception to the general statement that the budget process mirrors the legislative process. Budget reconciliation is an element of the Budget Control Act, which will be discussed below. Also included below is a glossary of budget terminology.

Our discussion will begin with a general description of budget formulation. This will be followed by a chart outlining budget preparation on a step-by-step basis for both Congress and the Executive Branch.

It should be noted at the outset that the discussion here is highly simplified. Those who closely follow the annual budget ritual know that it can be a complex and convoluted process, typically with the Congress and Executive Branch at loggerheads with each other and often fierce budget battles going on within the Congress itself. But budget decision-making is at the heart of how our Government functions, and for this reason it is vitally important that one have a basic understanding of the process by which spending and revenue decisions are arrived at. It is hoped that the material presented here will assist in that understanding.

INTRODUCTION TO THE FEDERAL BUDGET

Congress generally follows a two-step legislative process. First, it legislates programs as proposed by its various standing committees (i.e., Banking & Finance Committee, Energy & Commerce Committee, Judiciary Committee, etc.). This is known as the authorization process. Then it funds them as recommended by the Appropriations Committees. House and Senate rules have been adopted to keep authorization and appropriation as separate and distinct steps. In practice, however, the situation is more complicated. Authorization bills may contain appropriations, and appropriation bills are sometimes passed *before* authorization bills, not the other way around as Congressional rules specify.

In the real world of budget formulation, the Appropriations Committees are able to establish policy and act in a substantive manner. Conversely, authorization committees have considerable power to force the hand of Appropriations Committees and, in some cases, even to appropriate.

The congressional budgetary process is the last phase, albeit the most significant one, of the much larger annual process through which federal spending levels are arrived at. Although the Congress is the constitutionality prescribed trustee of the power of the purse, the Executive Branch has evolved as at least an equal partner in federal spending decisions. The size and complexity of the federal budget has forced the Congress to delegate a large part of the initial task of budgeting to the Executive. Under current procedures, the President is required to submit annually, within 15 days after the Congress convenes, a proposed federal budget. This annual budget document is the culmination of a year of preparation by agency officials, who channel their budget requests through the cabinet level, and then in turn through the Office of Management and Budget, which brings the requests in line with the President's program. The Congress has the final say on spending levels, but of necessity, many decisions of the Executive are merely ratified.

Congress is not only in the business of allocating funds one year in advance. Funds for certain projects must be spread over many years. If, for instance, Congress approves funding for a 5-year water project at a total cost of $50 million, this would show up in the budget as $50 million in budget authority — money for all 5 years — and $10 million in outlays — money to be spent in the first year.

This difference between budget authority (i.e., amounts appropriated) and outlays must be kept in mind when considering the federal budget and the Congressional role in its formation. The Congress is each year faced with a budget largely composed of spending and receipts that are fixed by authorization and appropriation decisions of previous years, and thus not generally subject to review.

CONGRESSIONAL BUDGET PROCESS

In appropriating monies for authorized programs, what Congress acts upon is not, in the literal sense, actual expenditures but rather requests for budget authority. Government agencies are granted budget authority and they in turn make the actual expenditure of Government funds.

There are basically three overlapping processes at work in each Congressional budget cycle.

(1) The first phase, the authorization process, occurs when the standing legislative committees authorize the obligations of funds for specific programs. An authorization specifies the substance of the particular program and which agencies shall be responsible for implementing it, but the authorization (with certain exceptions) does not determine the dollar amount to be spent; this is a function of budget appropriations. Authorizing legislation can set an outside limit on the funds for a given program, or can authorize the appropriation of "such sums as may be necessary." Certain major programs are authorized annually, as in the case of the regular defense procurement bill, while others, as is often the case with such programs as farm price supports, are authorized for several years in advance.

(2) The second phase, the appropriations process, usually determines how much funding each department, agency or program is allotted. The House and Senate Appropriations Committees are charged with this responsibility but, as indicated, most detailed work is done in the Appropriations Subcommittees which have jurisdiction over specific departments and agencies involved. The Constitution requires that all revenue measures originate in the House of Representatives, and by tradition the House claims the right to originate all appropriations measures. The practical effect of this has been that the House Appropriations Committee has generally exercised the predominant voice in shaping spending bills, while the Senate Appropriations Committee has come to be viewed as a court of appeals by agencies that have lost funding battles in the House.

As indicated, in the real world of budget politics, the two-step authorization and appropriation process are often not followed. While both chambers of Congress have rules barring "legislation on an appropriations measure" (i.e., writing substantive policy guidelines for an agency or program into a money bill), this rule seems to be honored more in the breach than in the observance. One strategy to avoid the rule has been to "earmark" funds for certain purposes within agency funding. Another popular tactic has been to attach "riders", amendments barring funds except in certain narrow circumstances, to appropriations bills. A recent example of this was anti-abortion language attached to Labor/Health and Human Services funding. These tactics tend to blur the distinction between the authorization process, which focuses on policy goals, and the appropriations process, which is concerned with adequate spending levels.

(3) The third phase can be referred to as the budget resolution process, based on the fact that the overall Congressional budget takes the form of two annual concurrent resolutions on the budget. This phase of the budget process was added by the Congressional Budget and Impoundment Control Act of 1974,[1] which was designed to restore Congressional control over overall spending. Prior to enactment of the Budget Control Act, total federal spending was, more often than not, arrived at in a haphazard manner, the predictably chaotic result of a series of uncoordinated authorization measures, 13 annual appropriations bills, "backdoor" spending devices (see below), and various revenue-raising decisions. While the Act has not accomplished all it set out to, most agree that it has been an improvement.

Under the Budget Control Act, the Congress each year must pass a concurrent resolution on the budget, establishing the overall level of spending, revenues and corresponding deficit (or surplus), before considering any legislation authorizing new budget authority. In addition, the totals in the first budget resolution, which are "targets" for the fiscal year commencing October 1, are subdivided into the 19 federal spending functions, such as defense and health. A second budget resolution must also be approved each budget cycle prior to the beginning of the fiscal year, affirming or revising the targets of the first resolution. If the spending level envisioned in the first resolution is exceeded, the Congress can either increase the spending ceiling in the second resolution, or direct a reconciliation. The reconciliation provision allows the House and Senate to order a particular committee to bring a spending measure into line with the original spending estimates.

A key part of the Congressional budget process is a timetable which coordinates the authorization and appropriations cycles with the overall Congressional budget enacted by the first and second budget resolutions. This timetable is an attempt to discipline the previously haphazard authorization and appropriations processes. In addition, it channels legislative activity for the entire Congress, forcing the committees to hold hearings, markup bills, and report legislation prior to the May 15th budget deadline (see below). In early months of each the Congressional session, activity centers in the various committees; in late spring and summer it shifts to the floor of both chambers, and to the passage of the coming year's spending legislation.

[1]Public Law 93-344.

The timetable laid down in the Budget Act is as follows:

BUDGET TIMETABLE[1]

On or before:	Action to be completed:
November 10	President submits current services budget.
15th day after Congress meets	President submits his budget to Congress.
March 15	Committees and joint committees submit reports to Budget Committees.
April 1	Congressional Budget Office submits report to Budget Committees.
April 15	Budget Committees report first concurrent resolution on the budget to their Houses.
May 15	Committees report bills and resolutions authorizing new budget authority.
May 15	Congress completes action on first concurrent resolution on the Budget.
7th day after Labor Day	Congress completes action on bills and resolutions providing new budget authority and new spending authority.
September 15	Congress completes action on second required concurrent resolution on the budget.
September 25	Congress completes action on reconciliation bill or resolution, or both, implementing second required concurrent resolution.
October 1	Fiscal year begins.

_____

[1]See Chart beginning on page 71.

NOVEMBER 10

The first step in the budget timetable is the submission by the President of the Current Services Budget, projecting federal spending for the coming 5 years on the basis of continuing current programs, excluding any program initiatives. The Congressional Budget Office (CBO), established by the Budget Act to supply bipartisan budget data and analysis, also prepares a similar 5-year budget projection. All such budget projections are contingent on certain assumptions — rate of growth in GNP, levels of inflation and unemployment, etc.

15 DAYS AFTER CONGRESS CONVENES

Following the submission of the President's budget, usually in late January, the Senate and House Budget Committees begin hearings to examine the President's economic assumptions and spending priorities, in preparation for drafting the first concurrent resolution on the budget.

MARCH 15

Soon after the President submits his budget, the authorization and appropriations committees begin to hold hearings on various components of the budget. By March 15th they must report to the Budget Committees their estimates of new budget authority to be enacted for the upcoming fiscal year. Some committees actually hold formal mark-up sessions to draft these budget reports, and occasionally the reports are of sufficient detail to be a good forecast of the committees' legislative priorities. The reports are used by the Budget Committees as an early warning system — to gauge the total and functional spending estimates contained in the first budget resolution.

APRIL 1

By April 1st the Congressional Budget Office (CBO) prepares a report outlining alternative national spending patterns, which is used in drafting the first budget resolution. The CBO report presents the Congress with spending scenarios above and below the President's.

APRIL 15

By April 15, the Budget Committees of each chamber must file their reports accompanying the first budget resolution. The first budget resolution establishes targets for: (1) the appropriate level of total outlays (money to be spent in the coming fiscal year) and total new budget authority (money to be spent in the coming fiscal year and in future fiscal years) both in the aggregate and by functional category; (2) the appropriate budget surplus or deficit; (3) the recommended level of federal revenues; (4) the appropriate level of public debt.

MAY 15

The dual May 15th budget deadline (see Budget Timetable above) is probably the most significant of the entire process. Under the first of this two-pronged requirement, all legislation proposing new budget authority must be reported by May 15. If a committee fails to meet this deadline, the legislation cannot be considered by the House or Senate unless a waiver is reported by the House Rules Committee or the Senate Budget Committee, respectively.

The administration is required to make requests for authorizing legislation a year in advance of the May 15th reporting deadline. This allows the committees a full year to deal with administration requests for authorizations. In addition, just as the authorizing bills must be reported by May 15th, the appropriations bills cannot be reported before this date. In theory, this serves to neatly segment the authorization and appropriations phases, but naturally there is some overlap, especially when the spending bills come to the House and Senate floors.

Congress must complete action on the first budget resolution to satisfy the second part of the May 15th deadline. Until the first budget resolution has been finalized, setting a "target" spending ceiling and revenue floor for the fiscal year, neither house can consider any spending or revenue measure which would take effect in that fiscal year.

7TH DAY AFTER LABOR DAY

By the 7th day after Labor Day, the Congress is required to complete action on all regular authorization and appropriations measures. The only exception to this rule is consideration of bills which have been delayed because necessary authorizing legislation has not been enacted in time. Sticking to this deadline assumes importance when one recalls that

Congress over the past decades has been extremely lax in passing spending measures before entering a new fiscal year. This has forced departments and agencies to exist on "continuing resolutions" — the prior year's funding levels — and barred the implementation of new programs.

SEPTEMBER 15

While there is no deadline for the reporting of the second budget resolution, it normally occurs before the annual August recess (or immediately thereafter), and must be finalized by September 15th. The total and functional spending levels in the first resolution are "targets," but these figures in the second resolution are "binding." This has the effect of "locking in" a congressional spending ceiling and a revenue floor. Once the second budget resolution is in place, no legislation can be passed which would breach these limits, unless Congress passes a subsequent budget resolution.

SEPTEMBER 25

Provision was made in the Budget Act, in the so-called reconciliation process, for the Congress to direct committees to bring spending and revenue measures into line. The committees can be directed to report bills or resolutions embodying the changes, and the Congress must complete action on these by September 25. The Congress cannot adjourn until a second budget resolution and any reconciliation measures are cleared.

OCTOBER 1

The fiscal year begins October 1. For example, Fiscal Year 1982 began October 1, 1981.

BUDGET COMMITTEES AND CONGRESSIONAL BUDGET OFFICE

Several new budget institutions were established by the Budget Act. Under the Act, budget committees were set up in the House and Senate to implement the new budget procedures, draft and report the first and second budget resolutions, and monitor congressional spending actions. Another institution, the Congressional Budget Office (CBO), was formed to act as a counterweight to the resources of the Office of Management and Budget (OMB), by supplying the Congress with impartial budgetary data and policy analysis.

The primary responsibility of the Budget Committees is to report and see passed the two annual budget resolutions. During the interim, between the passage of both resolutions, the budget committees also monitor the individual authorization, appropriations, and revenue decisions taken by the Congress. This "scorekeeping" function keeps the Congress informed of progress it is making towards meeting its budget targets. Status reports are published weekly by the Senate Budget Committee (during legislative session) and periodically by the House Budget Committee.

Both committees are standing legislative committees. The Senate's 16 members are chosen through normal Senate procedures, while the 25 House members are composed of 5 members from each of the Appropriations and Ways and Means Committees, 13 from other standing committees and one each from the majority and minority leadership. In addition, the membership of the House Budget Committee differs from other standing committees in that it is rotating. No member can serve more than 2 terms (4 years) during any 10-year period. Since the new congressional budget process was essentially superimposed over the authorization and appropriations cycles, the Budget Committee chairmen have played a large part in carving out an institutional role for the committees.

The Congressional Budget Office provides the Congress with spending projections of all authorizing legislation reported in either the House or Senate.

CBO is required to prepare a report to be used as a comparative tool in drafting the first budget resolution. CBO is governed by a Director, appointed to a four-year term by the Speaker of the House and President Pro Tem of the Senate on the advice of the Budget Committees.

BACKDOOR SPENDING

Congress has increasingly resorted over the past few decades to forms of spending which circumvent the traditional two step congressional spending process. The term "backdoor spending" refers to spending which by-passes the regular appropriations process. Thus, while there is a general rule that spending for a program cannot result where there is not both a specific authorization, and an appropriation of funds to carry out the program, the area of backdoor spending has evolved as a gaping loophole. By 1974 backdoor spending accounted for 40 percent of all federal outlays.

The term backdoor spending is actually an umbrella category including a variety of spending devices. One device, referred to as an entitlement, includes programs such as food stamps and veterans disability benefits, where the government is obligated to extend benefits to all individuals meeting certain criteria. Another type of backdoor spending, known as borrowing authority, allows government agencies such as the Commodity Credit Corporation, to operate by borrowing either from the Treasury or directly from the public. Contract authority refers to yet another type of backdoor spending. Under this method an authorization, for instance, the Federal Water Pollution Control Act, provides a lump sum in contract authority for sewage treatment facilities over several years. In each of these cases, funds are obligated in advance of a formal appropriation.

The Congress began to curb abuse of backdoor spending in the 1960's, but not until the Congressional Budget & Impoundment Control Act of 1974, did Congress deal systematically with the problem. The Act closed the door on all new borrowing and contract authority by requiring this form of spending to go through the appropriations process. All new entitlement legislation which breaches the limits for a particular function (national defense, health, etc.), is automatically referred by the Act to the Appropriations Committee, which can reduce the amount to bring it within the spending ceiling. The Budget Act exempts certain favored legislation from these stipulations, including social security and revenue sharing measures.

One other mechanism, known as a tax expenditure, is another form of backdoor spending device. A tax expenditure or tax subsidy decreases the tax liability of a particular group — homeowners, businesses who invest in new plants and equipment, and oil and gas firms who engage in exploration. In this sense, they are not only tax measures, but a form of backdoor spending, because neither the authorizing committees nor the appropriations committees have any jurisdiction over how much is spent — in the form of lost tax dollars.

IMPOUNDMENT

Title X of the Budget Act established a procedure for Congressional involvement in all executive impoundments, rescissions and deferrals. In the case of a rescission — an outright cancellation of budget authority passed by Congress — the President must submit a message detailing the proposed rescission, the affected agency, reasons for rescission, and the estimated fiscal and program impact of the proposed action. If Congress does not pass a rescission bill (or joint resolution) within 45 days of continuous session, the President must release the funds. In this case, the burden is on the President to convince the Congress to approve his action.

In the case of a deferral — a delay in budget authority not beyond a year — the President again must submit a special message indicating the reasons for the proposed delay in spending. Unless either House passes an impoundment resolution overruling the President's action, it takes effect.

THE EXECUTIVE BRANCH BUDGET

Each January, as indicated, the President sends a proposed Federal budget to Congress for the fiscal year that begins the next October 1. The Office of Management and Budget (OMB) prepares the budget proposals for the President and has the responsibility within the executive branch for supervising expenditures once a federal budget has been enacted into law.

Early in the summer, prior to the President's January budget proposals sent to Congress, the OMB sends budget ceilings to the agencies of the Executive Branch, reflecting the President's positions. In September, the agencies then give OMB their plans for programs and their estimates of financial requirements for the year under consideration and for two additional years beyond that.

A series of charts detailing the major steps in the formulation of both the President's budget and the Congressional budget is given below, beginning on page 71. This is preceded by a glossary of budget terms.

OMB then develops a preliminary budget outlook as its analysts complete their reviews of the agencies' programs, detailing their projections for the future of those programs and identifying major issues for discussions with representatives of the agencies.

During the budget process, the President's economic advisers again assess the economy and prepare a revised estimate of revenues and spending plans for the President. After this, and based on any changes the President has made in his preliminary decisions, OMB sends "directive letters," that set spending levels and priorities, to each department and agency. Recipients can appeal directly to the President for changes they believe should be made in OMB's decisions, but most disagreements are settled between the Director of OMB and the head of the department or agency involved.

The President, in late December, makes his final decisions on the budget. The document is then printed, and the President prepares his budget message, which usually goes to the Congress in mid-January.

The budget proposes to Congress specific levels of budget authority and actual outlays for all government agencies and functions. It presents in detail the basis for Administration programs. Now it is up to the Congress to deliberate and act, as described above.

Congress can approve, modify or reject the President's budget proposals. It can change funding levels, eliminate proposals, or add programs not requested by the President, and it acts on legislation determining taxes and other means of increasing or decreasing receipts, as well as stimulating or slowing down the overall economy or certain segments of it.

The Congressional budget deadlines have been described above. Ideally, when the new fiscal year begins on October 1, the budget has been agreed on and is in place. Should the timetable slip, Congress can enact a "continuing resolution" to provide money for any agency whose appropriations have not yet been approved.

MAJOR OMB PUBLICATIONS

The following useful publications are available (at a charge) from the Superintendent of Documents, Government Printing Office, Washington, D.C. 20401.

• *The Budget of the United States Government,* contains the information that most users of the budget would normally need, including the Budget Message of the President.

This text presents an overview of the President's budget proposals, including explanations of spending programs, funding, receipts and the relationship of the budget to the economy.

- *The Budget of the United States Government — Appendix,* contains detailed information on the various appropriations and funds which comprise the budget. Here may be found the most itemized information of any of the budget documents, i.e., an agency-by-agency breakdown of all costs, accompanied by budget tables and explanations of work to be performed.

- *Special Analyses, Budget of the United States Government,* contains special analyses which highlight specified program areas or provide other significant presentations of Federal data. It covers government finances affecting education, manpower, health, income security, crime reduction, and other areas of government concern.

- *The United States Budget in Brief,* a pamphlet providing a concise and less technical overview of the budget, offers a variety of charts as well as summary and historical tables on the Federal budget and debt.

- *The Catalogue of Federal Domestic Assistance,* the most comprehensive and authoritative compilation available of the more than 1,000 Federal assistance programs.

- Berman, Larry. *The Office of Management and Budget and the Presidency, 1921-1979.* Princeton, Princeton University Press (1979), 130p.

GLOSSARY OF BUDGET TERMS*

ACCRUAL BASIS OF ACCOUNTING

A method of accounting in which revenues are recognized in the period earned and costs are recognized in the period incurred, regardless of when payment is received or made. (See also CASH BASIS OF ACCOUNTING.)

ACTIVITY

Any project, task, or process required to carry out a program. A combination of several activities, such as research and development, training of personnel, and distribution of information, may be elements in a particular program. Activities constituting a program vary with the nature and purpose of the program.

ADVANCE APPROPRIATION

An appropriation provided by the Congress for use in a fiscal year, or more, beyond the fiscal year for which the appropriation act is passed, e.g., the 1976 appropriation for use in fiscal year 1976 for the Washington Metropolitan Area Transit Authority contained in the Department of Transportation and Related Agencies Appropriation Act, 1975, which was passed on August 28, 1974. Advance appropriations allow State and local governments and others sufficient time to develop plans with assurance of future Federal funding. An advance appropriation is sometimes mistakenly referred to as "forward funding" which permits an agency to obligate funds in the current year for the operation of programs in subsequent fiscal years. (See also ADVANCE FUNDING and FORWARD FUNDING.)

ADVANCE FUNDING

Authority provided in an appropriations act to obligate and disburse during a fiscal year from the succeeding year's appropriation. The funds so obligated are added to the budget authority for the fiscal year and deducted from the budget authority of the succeeding fiscal year. The appropriation language usually states the date after which the funds of the succeeding year may be obligated. The "Public Assistance" appropriation account, HEW, is an example. (See ADVANCE APPROPRIATION and FORWARD FUNDING.).

AGENCY

Any department, office, commission, authority, administration, board, Government-owned corporation, or other independent establishment of any branch of the Government of the United States.

AGENCY DEBT

See FEDERAL DEBT

AGENCY MISSIONS

Those responsibilities for meeting national needs assigned to a specific agency. Agency missions are expressed in terms of the purpose to be served by the programs authorized to carry out functions or subfunctions which, by law, are the responsibility of that agency and its component organizations. (See section 201 of the Budget and Accounting Act, 1921, as amended. (See also ACTIVITY and NATIONAL NEEDS.)

ALLOCATION

This term has two definitions: (1) For purposes of Government accounting, an allocation is the amount of obligational authority transferred from one agency, bureau, or account to another agency, bureau, or account that is set aside in a transfer appropriation account to carry out the purposes of the parent appropriation or fund. For example, allocations are made when one or more agencies share the administration of a program for which appropriations are made to only one of the agencies or to the President. (2) For purposes of section 302(a) of the Congressional Budget Act of 1974, an allocation is the distribution of the total budget outlays or total new budget authority in a concurrent resolution on the budget to the various committees having spending responsibilities.

ALLOTMENT

Authority delegated by the head or other authorized employee of an agency to agency employees to incur obligations within a specified amount pursuant to OMB apportionment or reapportionment action or other statutory authority making funds available for obligation.

ALLOWANCES

Amounts included in the President's budget request or projections to cover possible additional proposals, such as statutory pay increases and contingencies for relatively uncontrollable programs and other requirements. As used in a concurrent resolution on the budget, allowances represent a special functional classification designed to include amounts to cover possible requirements, such as civilian pay raises and contingencies, until they occur or become firm, at which point applicable amounts are distributed to the other appropriate functional classification(s).

---

*These definitions are reprinted from "Terms Used in The Budgetary Process," by the Comptroller General of the United States, July 1977 (GAO No. PAD-77-9).

APPORTIONMENT

A distribution by the Office of Management and Budget of amounts available for obligation in appropriation or fund accounts of the executive branch. The distribution makes amounts available on the basis of time periods (usually quarterly), programs, activities, projects, objects, or combinations thereof. The apportionment system is intended to achieve an effective and orderly use of funds.

DEFICIENCY APPORTIONMENT

A distribution of available budgetary resources for the fiscal year that anticipates the need for supplemental budget authority. Such apportionments may only be made under conditions provided in 31 U.S.C. 665(e) and 665(a). The issuance of a deficiency apportionment does not authorize the agency head to incur a deficit.

APPROPRIATION

An authorization by an act of the Congress that permits Federal agencies to incur obligations and to make payments out of the Treasury for specified purposes. An appropriation usually follows enactment of authorizing legislation. An appropriation act is the most common means of providing budget authority (see BUDGET AUTHORITY) but in some cases the authorizing legislation itself provides the budget authority. (See BACKDOOR AUTHORITY.) Appropriations do not represent cash actually set aside in the Treasury for purposes specified in the appropriation act; they represent limitations of amounts which agencies may obligate during the time period specified in the respective appropriations acts. There are several types of appropriations that are not counted as budget authority, since they do not provide authority to incur additional obligations:

- —Appropriation to liquidate contract authority — congressional action to provide funds to pay obligations incurred against contract authority.
- —Appropriation to reduce outstanding debt — congressional action to provide funds for debt retirement.
- —Appropriation for refund of receipts.

APPROPRIATION (OR FUND) ACCOUNT

A summary account established in the Treasury for each appropriation and/or fund showing transactions to such accounts.

APPROPRIATION ACT

An act under the jurisdiction of the Committees on Appropriations which provides funds for Federal programs. At the time these definitions were published, there were 13 regular appropriation acts. There are also enacted from time to time supplemental appropriation acts.

APPROPRIATION LIMITATION

A statutory restriction in an appropriation act, which establishes the maximum amount which may be obligated and expended for specified purposes from an appropriation or other funds, such as special or trust funds.

AUTHORITY TO BORROW FROM THE TREASURY AND THE PUBLIC

See BORROWING AUTHORITY.

AUTHORIZATION (AUTHORIZING LEGISLATION)

Basic substantive legislation enacted by Congress which sets up or continues the legal operation of a Federal program or agency either indefinitely or for a specific period of time or sanctions a particular type of obligation or expenditure within a program. Such legislation is normally a prerequisite for subsequent appropriations or other kinds of budget authority to be contained in appropriation acts. It may limit the amount of budget authority to be provided subsequently or may authorize the appropriation of "such sums as may be necessary." In some instances budget authority may be provided in the authorization (see BACKDOOR AUTHORITY), which obviates the need for subsequent appropriations or requires only an appropriation to liquidate contract authority or reduce outstanding debt.

AUTHORIZING COMMITTEE

A standing committee of the House or Senate with jurisdiction over the subject matter of those laws, or parts of laws, that set up or continue the legal operations of Federal programs, agencies, or particular types of obligations within programs. The authorizing committee also has spending responsibility in those instances where the budget authority ("backdoor authority") is also provided in the basic substantive legislation.

BACKDOOR AUTHORITY

Budget authority provided in legislation outside the normal (appropriations committees) appropriations process. The most common forms of backdoor authority are borrowing authority and contract authority. In other cases (e.g., interest on the public debt), a permanent appropriation is provided that becomes available without any current action by the Congress. Section 401 of the Congressional Budget Act of 1974 specifies certain limits on the use of backdoor authority. Examples of accounts that

Permanent Authority

Budget authority that becomes available as the result of previously enacted legislation (substantive legislation or prior appropriation act) and does not require current action by the Congress. Authority created by such legislation is considered to be "current" in the first year in which it is provided and "permanent" in succeeding years. It is possible to distinguish between "fully permanent" authority (such as interest on the public debt), where no subsequent action is required, and "conditionally permanent" authority (such as general revenue sharing), where authority expires after a set period of time unless it is reenacted.

DETERMINATION OF AMOUNT

Definite Authority

Authority which is stated as a specific sum at the time the authority is granted. This includes authority stated as "not to exceed" a specified amount.

Indefinite Authority

Authority for which a specific sum is not stated but is to be determined by other factors, such as the receipts from a certain source or obligations incurred.

BUDGET DEFICIT

The amount by which the Government's budget outlays exceed its budget receipts for any given period. Deficits are financed primarily by Treasury borrowing from the public.

BUDGET OUTLAYS

See OUTLAYS

BUDGET RECEIPTS

Amounts received by the Federal Government from the public that arise from:

—The exercise of governmental or sovereign power (consisting primarily of tax revenues, but also including receipts from premiums of compulsory social insurance programs, court fines, certain license fees, and the like).
—Premiums from voluntary participants in Federal social insurance programs (such as deposits by States for unemployment insurance and for social security for their employees) that are closely related to compulsory social insurance programs.
—Gifts and contributions.

Excluded from budget receipts are OFFSETTING RECEIPTS, which are counted as deductions from budget authority and outlays rather than as budget receipts.

BUDGET SURPLUS

The amount by which the Government's budget receipts exceed its budget outlays for any given period.

BUDGET UPDATE

A statement summarizing amendments to or revisions in budget authority requested, estimated outlays, and estimated receipts for a fiscal year that has not been completed. The President may submit updates at any time but is required by the Congressional Budget Act of 1974 to transmit such statements to the Congress by April 10 and July 15 of each year.

BUDGET YEAR

See FISCAL YEAR

BUDGETARY RESERVES

Portions of budget authority set aside under authority of the Antideficiency Act (31 U.S.C. 665) as amended by the Impoundment Control Act of 1974, for contingencies or to effect savings whenever savings are made possible by or through changes in requirements or greater efficiency of operations. Section 1002 of the Impoundment Control Act of 1974 restricts the establishment of budgetary reserves and requires that all reserves be reported to the Congress. (See DEFERRAL OF BUDGET AUTHORITY.)

CASH BASIS OF ACCOUNTING

A method of accounting in which revenue is recognized at the time payment is received and costs are considered incurred at the time payment is made. (See also ACCRUAL BASIS OF ACCOUNTING.)

CHANGE IN SELECTED RESOURCES

An adjustment in the program and financing schedules of the President's budget appendix representing the bridge between program costs and obligations. It measures the aggregate increase or decrease in those assets and liabilities that have entered into obligations but have not yet become costs, or vice versa. (See COST BASED BUDGETING.) Details for computing "change in selected resources" are included in section 32.3 of OMB Circular A-11.

COLLECTIONS

Any moneys received by the Government. Depending upon the nature of the transaction, collections may be treated as budget receipts, offsetting collections, refunds, or credits to a deposit fund. (See BUDGET RECEIPTS, OFFSETTING COLLECTIONS, REFUNDS, DEPOSIT FUNDS.)

have backdoor authority are the Federal-aid highways trust fund, the Environmental Protection Agency's construction grants, and the social security trust funds.

BALANCED BUDGET

A budget in which receipts are equal to or greater than outlays. (See BUDGET DEFICIT and BUDGET SURPLUS.)

BALANCES OF BUDGET AUTHORITY

Balances may be classified as:

Unexpended Balance

The amount of budget authority unspent and still available for conversion into outlays in the future; the sum of the obligated and unobligated balances.

Obligated Balance

The amount of obligations already incurred for which payment has not yet been made. This balance can be carried forward indefinitely until the obligations are paid.

Unobligated Balance

The portion of budget authority that has not yet been obligated. In 1-year accounts the unobligated balance expires (ceases to be available for obligation) at the end of the fiscal year. In multiple-year accounts the unobligated balance may be carried forward and remain available for obligation for the period specified. In no-year accounts the unobligated balance is carried forward indefinitely until specifically rescinded by law or until the purposes for which it was provided have been accomplished.

BORROWING AUTHORITY

Statutory authority (substantive or appropriation) that permits a Federal agency to incure obligations and to make payments for specified purposes out of borrowed moneys. Section 401 of the Congressional Budget Act of 1974 limits new borrowing authority (except for certain instances) to such extent or in such amounts as are provided in appropriation acts. Borrowing authority, also called "authority to borrow from the Treasury and the Public," may be one of the following types:

Authority to Borrow From the Treasury

The legislative authority to borrow funds from the Treasury that are realized from the sale of public debt securities.

Authority to Borrow From the Public

The legislative authority to sell agency debt securities.

Authority to Borrow From the Treasury and the Public

A combination of the legislative authorities noted above.

BUDGET ACTIVITY

Categories included in the budget appendix for each appropriation and fund account which identify the services to be performed under the appropriation or fund for which the budget estimate (or request) is being made.

BUDGET AMENDMENT

A formal request submitted to the Congress by the President, after his formal budget transmittal but prior to completion of appropriation action by the Congress, that revises previous requests, such as the amount of budget authority.

BUDGET AUTHORITY

Authority provided by law to enter into obligations which will result in immediate or future outlays involving Government funds, except that such term does not include authority to insure or guarantee the repayment of indebtedness incurred by another person or government. The basic forms of budget authority are appropriations, contract authority, and borrowing authority. Budget authority may be classified by the period of availability (1-year, multiple-year, no-year), by the timing of congressional action (current or permanent), or by the manner of determining the amount available (definite or indefinite).

PERIOD OF AVAILABILITY

One-year (Annual Authority)

Budget authority that is available for obligation only during a specified fiscal year and expires at the end of that time.

Multiple-year Authority

Budget authority that is available for a specified period of time in excess of 1 fiscal year.

No-year Authority

Budget authority that remains available for obligation for an indefinite period of time, usually until the objectives for which the authority was made available are attained.

TIMING OF CONGRESSIONAL ACTION

Current Authority

Budget authority enacted by Congress in or immediately preceding the fiscal year in which it becomes available.

CONCURRENT RESOLUTION ON THE BUDGET

A resolution passed by both Houses of Congress, but not requiring the signature of the President, setting forth, reaffirming, or revising the congressional budget for the United States Government for a fiscal year. There are two such resolutions required preceding each fiscal year. The first required concurrent resolution, due by May 15, establishes the congressional budget. The second required concurrent resolution, due by September 15, reaffirms or revises it. Other concurrent resolutions for a fiscal year may be adopted at any time following the first required concurrent resolution for that fiscal year.

CONGRESSIONAL BUDGET

The budget as set forth by Congress in a concurrent resolution on the budget. These resolutions shall include:

(1) the appropriate level of total budget outlays and of total new budget authority,
(2) an estimate of budget outlays and new budget authority for each major functional category, for contingencies, and for undistributed offsetting receipts based on allocations of the appropriate level of total budget outlays and of total new budget authority.
(3) the amount, if any, of the surplus or deficit in the budget,
(4) the recommended level of Federal revenues, and
(5) the appropriate level of the public debt.

CONTINGENT LIABILITY

A conditional commitment which may become an actual liability because of a future event beyond the control of the Government. Contingent liabilities include such items as guaranteed loans and insured bank deposits.

CONTINUING RESOLUTION

Legislation enacted by the Congress to provide budget authority for specific ongoing activities in cases where the regular fiscal year appropriation for such activities has not been enacted by the beginning of the fiscal year. The continuing resolution usually specifies a maximum rate at which the agency may incur obligations, based on the rate of the prior year, the President's budget request, or an appropriation bill passed by either or both Houses of the Congress.

CONTRACT AUTHORITY

A form of budget authority under which contracts or other obligations may be entered into in advance of an appropriation or in excess of amounts otherwise available in a revolving fund. Contract authority must be funded by a subsequent appropriation or the use of revolving fund collections to liquidate the obligations. Appropriations to liquidate contract authority are not classified as budget authority since they are not available for obligation. Section 401 of the Congressional Budget Act of 1974 limits new contract authority with few exceptions, to such extent or in such amounts as are provided in appropriation acts.

CONTROLLABILITY

The ability under existing law to control budget authority or outlays during a given fiscal year. "Relatively uncontrollable" usually refers to spending that cannot be increased or decreased without changes in existing substantive law. The largest part of such spending is the result of open-ended programs and fixed costs, such as social security and benefits, but also includes payments due under obligations incurred during prior years.

COST-BASED BUDGETING

Budgeting in terms of costs to be incurred, i.e., the resources to be consumed in carrying out a program regardless of when the funds to acquire the resources were obligated or paid. Cost-based budgeting, in addition to reflecting the obligational requirements for the program, presents the cost of what is planned to be accomplished. (Obligation-based budgeting is expressed in terms of obligations to be incurred, regardless of when the resources acquired are to be consumed.) When the financing schedules in the appendix to the President's budget state the "program by activities" in terms of costs, an adjusting entry is required to arrive at total obligations. (See CHANGE IN SELECTED RESOURCES.)

CROSSWALK

The expression of the relationship between one set of classifications and another, such as between appropriation accounts and authorizing legislation or between the budget functional structure and the congressional committee spending jurisdictions.

CURRENT AUTHORITY

See BUDGET AUTHORITY.

CURRENT POLICY BUDGET

Projections of the estimated budget authority and outlays for the upcoming fiscal year to operate Federal programs at the level implied by enacted appropriations and authorizations for the current fiscal year without policy changes, but adjusted for inflation, changes in the numbers and kinds of beneficiaries, and in some instances to reflect the continuation of certain programs scheduled to terminate.

CURRENT SERVICES ESTIMATES

Estimated budget authority and outlays for the upcoming fiscal year based on continuation of existing levels of service, i.e., assuming that all programs and activities will be carried on at the same level as in the fiscal year in progress and without policy changes in such programs and activities. These estimates of budget authority and outlays, accompanied by the underlying economic and programmatic assumptions upon which they are based (such as the rate of inflation, the rate of real economic growth, the unemployment rate, program caseloads, and pay increases), are required to be transmitted by the President to the Congress by November 10 of each year.

CURRENT YEAR

See FISCAL YEAR.

DEBT HELD BY THE PUBLIC

See FEDERAL DEBT.

DEBT SUBJECT TO STATUTORY LIMITATION

See FEDERAL DEBT.

DEFERRAL OF BUDGET AUTHORITY

Any action or inaction by any officer or employee of the United States that withholds, delays, or effectively precludes that obligation or expenditure of budget authority, including the establishment of reserves under the Antideficiency Act as amended by the Impoundment Control Act. (See BUDGETARY RESERVES.) Section 1013 of the Impoundment Control Act of 1974 requires a special message from the President to the Congress reporting a proposed deferral of budget authority. Deferrals may not extend beyond the end of the fiscal year in which the message reporting the deferral is transmitted and may be overturned by the passage of an impoundment resolution by either House of Congress. (See IMPOUNDMENT RESOLUTION.)

DEFICIENCY APPORTIONMENT

See APPORTIONMENT.

DEFICIENCY APPROPRIATION

An appropriation made to an expired account to cover obligations incurred in excess of the available budget authority.

DEFINITE AUTHORITY

See BUDGET AUTHORITY.

DEOBLIGATION

A downward adjustment of previously recorded obligations. This may be attributable to cancellation of a project or contract, price revisions, or corrections of amounts previously recorded as obligations.

DEPOSIT FUNDS

Accounts established to facilitate the accounting for collections that are either (a) held in suspense temporarily and later refunded or paid into some other fund of the Government upon administrative or legal determination as to the proper disposition thereof or (b) held by the Government as banker or agent for others and paid out at the discretion of the depositor. These accounts are not included in the budget totals and they are not available for expenses of the Government, although they do provide a means of financing the budget.

DIRECT LOANS

Outlays, all or part of which are contracted to be repaid with or without interest. Sales of Federal assets on credit terms of more than 90 days' duration are also classified as direct loans.

DISBURSEMENTS

In budgetary usage, gross disbursements represent the amount of checks issued, cash, or other payments made, less refunds received. Net disbursements represent gross disbursements less income collected and credited to the appropriation or fund account, such as amounts received for goods and services provided. (See EXPENDITURES and OUTLAYS.)

ENTITLEMENT AUTHORITY

Legislation that requires the payment of benefits to any person or government meeting the requirements established by such law, e.g., social security benefits and veterans' pensions. Section 401 of the Congressional Budget Act of 1974 places certain restrictions on the enactment of new entitlement authority.

EXPENDITURES

A term generally used interchangeably with outlays. (See OUTLAYS.) (At one time, the term was used to describe one form of outlays, the other being "net lending." This usage is now obsolete.)

EXPIRED APPROPRIATION

An appropriation that is no longer available for obligation but is still available for payment of existing obligations. (See "M" ACCOUNTS.)

FEDERAL DEBT

Federal debt consists of public debt and agency debt.

Public Debt

That portion of the Federal debt incurred when the Treasury Department or Federal Financing Bank (FFB) borrows funds directly from the public or another fund or account. To avoid double counting, FFB borrowing from Treasury is not included in public debt. (The Treasury borrowing required to obtain the money to lend FFB is already part of the public debt.)

Agency Debt

That portion of the Federal debt incurred when a Federal agency authorized by law, other than Treasury or the Federal Financing Bank (FFB), borrows funds directly from the public or another fund or account. To avoid double counting, agency borrowing from Treasury or the FFB and Federal fund advances to trust funds are not included in the Federal debt. (The Treasury or FFB borrowing required to obtain the money to lend to the agency is already part of the public debt.) Agency debt may be incurred by agencies within the Federal budget (such as the Tennessee Valley Authority) or by off-budget Federal entities (such as the Postal Service). Debt of Government-sponsored, privately owned enterprises (such as the Federal National Mortgage Association) is not included in the Federal debt.

There are three basic concepts or tabulations of Federal debt: gross Federal debt, debt held by the public, and debt subject to statutory limit.

Gross Federal Debt

The sum of all public and agency debt issues outstanding.

Debt Held by the Public

That part of the gross Federal debt held by the public. (The Federal Reserve System is included in "the public" for this purpose.) Debt held by Government trust funds (e.g., Social Security Trust Fund), revolving funds, and off-budget Federal entities is excluded from debt held by the public.

Debt Subject to Statutory Limit

Defined by the Second Liberty Bond Act of 1917, as amended. At present virtually all public debt, but only a small portion of agency debt, is included in debt subject to statutory limit.

FEDERAL FUND ACCOUNTS

Accounts in which the Government credits receipts which it collects, owns, and uses solely for its purposes. They are composed of two classes of receipt accounts — general fund receipt accounts and special fund receipt accounts — and four classes of appropriation (expenditure) or fund accounts — general fund appropriations, special fund appropriations, public enterprise revolving funds, and intragovernmental funds.

General Fund Receipt Accounts

Accounts credited with all receipts that are not earmarked by law for a specific purpose.

Special Fund Receipt Accounts

Accounts credited with receipts from specific sources that are earmarked by law for a specific purpose.

General Fund Appropriation Accounts

Accounts established to record amounts appropriated by the Congress to be expended for the general support of the Government.

Special Fund Appropriation Accounts

Accounts established to record appropriated amounts of special fund receipts to be expended for special programs in accordance with specific provisions of law.

Public Enterprise Revolving Fund Accounts

Funds authorized by Congress to be credited with receipts, primarily from the public, that are generated by, and earmarked to finance, a continuing cycle of business-type operations.

Intragovernmental Fund Accounts

Accounts established to facilitate financing transactions within and between Federal agencies. These funds may be classified as intragovernmental revolving funds or management funds.

Intragovernmental Revolving Fund Accounts

Funds authorized by law to carry out a cycle of intragovernmental business-type operations. These funds are credited with offsetting collections from other agencies and accounts.

Management Fund Accounts

Funds authorized by law to credit collections from two or more appropriations in order to finance a common purpose or project not involving a continuing cycle of business-type operations.

FEDERAL INTRAFUND TRANSACTIONS

See OFFSETTING RECEIPTS.

FISCAL POLICY

Federal Government policies with respect to taxes, spending, and debt management, intended to promote the Nation's economic goals, particularly with respect to employment, gross national product, price level stability, and equilibrium in balance of payments. The budget process is a major vehicle for determining and implementing Federal fiscal policy. The other major component of Federal economic policy is MONETARY POLICY, defined in the section on economic terms.

FISCAL YEAR

Any yearly accounting period, without regard to its relationship to a calendar year. The fiscal year for the Federal Government begins on October 1 and ends on September 30. The fiscal year is designated by the calendar year in which it ends; e.g., fiscal year 1977 is the fiscal year ending September 30, 1977. (Prior to fiscal year 1977 the fiscal year began on July 1 and ended on June 30.)

Budget Year

The fiscal year for which the budget is being considered; the fiscal year following the current year.

Current Year

The fiscal year in progress.

Past Year

The fiscal year immediately preceding the current year; the last completed fiscal year.

FOREIGN CURRENCY ACCOUNT

An account established in the Treasury for foreign currency that is acquired without payment of United States dollars, primarily in payment for commodities (such as through the Agricultural Trade Development Assistance Act, P.L. 480). These currencies may be expended without charge to dollar appropriations. They may be available for obligation without further congressional action, or Congress may appropriate these foreign currencies. (See also SPECIAL FOREIGN CURRENCY PROGRAM APPROPRIATION.)

FORWARD FUNDING

The obligation of funds in one fiscal year (e.g., the awarding of a contract and establishment of a letter of credit) for the financing of ongoing grantee programs during the succeeding year. For example, in the "Higher Education" appropriation account, Office of Education, HEW, student loan funds are obligated at the end of the fiscal year for student loans to be made in the following year. (See also ADVANCE APPROPRIATION and ADVANCE FUNDING.)

FULL EMPLOYMENT BUDGET

The estimated receipts, outlays, and surplus or deficit that would occur if the economy were continually operating at a rate defined as being at full capacity (traditionally defined as a certain percentage unemployment rate for the civilian labor force).

FUNCTION
(FUNCTIONAL CLASSIFICATION)

The Congressional Budget Act of 1974 requires the Congress to estimate outlays, budget authority, and tax expenditures for each function. The functional classification is a means of presenting budget authority, outlay, and tax expenditure data in terms of the principal purposes that Federal programs are intended to serve. Each account is generally placed in the single function (e.g., national defense, health) that best represents its major purpose, regardless of the agency administering the program. Functions are generally subdivided into narrower categories called subfunctions.

GENERAL FUND ACCOUNTS

See FEDERAL FUND ACCOUNTS.

GOVERNMENT-SPONSORED ENTERPRISES

Enterprises with completely private ownership, such as Federal land banks and Federal home loan banks, established and chartered by the Federal Government to perform specialized functions. These enterprises are not included in the budget totals, but financial information on their operations is published in a separate part of the appendix to the President's budget.

GRANTS-IN-AID

For purposes of the budget, grants-in-aid consist of budget outlays by the Federal Government to support State or local programs of governmental service to the public. Grants do not include purchases from State or local governments (i.e., payments for research or support of Federal prisoners).

GROSS FEDERAL DEBT

See FEDERAL DEBT.

GUARANTEED LOANS

Loans for which the Federal Government guarantees in whole or in part the repayment of principal and/or interest.

IDENTIFICATION CODE

An 11-digit number assigned to each appropriation or fund account included in the budget. The identification code identifies the agency, the appropriation or fund account symbol, the timing of the transmittal (regular, supplemental), the type of fund (general, special), and the functional classification of each account (see FUNCTION).

IMPOUNDMENT

Any action or inaction by an officer or employee of the United States that precludes the obligation or expenditure of budget authority provided by the Congress. (See DEFERRAL OF BUDGET AUTHORITY and RESCISSION.)

IMPOUNDMENT RESOLUTION

A resolution of the House of Representatives or the Senate disapproving a deferral of budget authority set forth in a special message ordinarily transmitted by the President under section 1013 of the Impoundment Control Act of 1974. Passage of an impoundment resolution by either House of Congress has the effect of overturning the deferral and requires that such budget authority be made available for obligation.

INDEFINITE AUTHORITY

See BUDGET AUTHORITY.

INTRABUDGETARY TRANSACTIONS

See OFFSETTING RECEIPTS.

INTRAFUND TRANSACTIONS

See OFFSETTING RECEIPTS.

INTRAGOVERNMENTAL FUND ACCOUNTS

See FEDERAL FUND ACCOUNTS.

INTRAGOVERNMENTAL REVOLVING FUND ACCOUNTS

See FEDERAL FUND ACCOUNTS.

INTRAGOVERNMENTAL TRANSACTIONS

See OFFSETTING RECEIPTS.

LIQUIDATION OF CONTRACT AUTHORITY

See APPROPRIATION, CONTRACT AUTHORITY.

"M" ACCOUNT

Unliquidated obligations under an appropriation are transferred to (merged into) an "M" account at the end of the second full fiscal year following expiration. The "M" account remains available for the payment of the unliquidated obligations charged to various-year appropriation accounts.

MANAGEMENT FUND ACCOUNTS

See FEDERAL FUND ACCOUNTS.

MISSION

See AGENCY MISSION.

MULTIPLE-YEAR AUTHORITY

See BUDGET AUTHORITY.

NATIONAL NEEDS

Those Federal functions which describe the end purposes being served by budget authority, outlays, and tax expenditures, without regard to the means that may be chosen to meet those purposes. National needs, in current budgetary usage, may be assumed to be synonymous with "function."

NEW OBLIGATIONAL AUTHORITY

This term is now obsolete and has been replaced by the term "budget authority." (At one time the term was used to distinguish one of two types of budget authority — the other being "loan authority," which is also obsolete.)

NO-YEAR AUTHORITY

See BUDGET AUTHORITY.

OBJECT CLASSIFICATION

A uniform classification identifying the transactions of the Federal Government by the nature of the goods or services purchased (such as personnel compensation, supplies and materials, or equipment) without regard to the agency involved or the purpose of the programs for which they are used. (General instructions are provided in OMB Circular No. A-12).

OBLIGATIONS

Amounts of orders placed, contracts awarded, services rendered, or other commitments made by Federal agencies during a given period, which will require outlays during the same or some future period. (See 31 U.S.C. 200.)

OFF-BUDGET FEDERAL ENTITIES

Entities, federally owned in whole or in part, whose transactions have been excluded from the budget totals under provisions of law, e.g:, the Federal Financing Bank. The fiscal activities of these entities are not included in either budget authority or outlay totals, but are presented in a separate part of the budget appendix and as memorandum items in various tables in the budget.

OFFSETTING COLLECTIONS

Moneys received by the Government as a result of business-type transactions with the public (sale of goods and services) or as a result of a payment from one Government account to another. Such collections are netted in determining budget outlays. (See OFFSETTING RECEIPTS and REIMBURSEMENTS.)

OFFSETTING RECEIPTS

All collections deposited into receipt accounts that are offset against budget authority and outlays rather than reflected as budget receipts in computing budget totals. Under current budgetary usage, cash collections not deposited into receipt accounts (such as revolving fund receipts and reimbursements) are deducted from outlays at the account level. These transactions are offsetting collections but are not classified as "offsetting receipts."

Offsetting receipts are generally deducted at the budget function or subfunction level and from agency budget authority and outlays. In three cases — employer share of employee retirement, intragovernmental interest received by trust funds, and rents and royalties from the Outer Continental Shelf lands — the deductions, referred to as UNDISTRIBUTED OFFSETTING RECEIPTS, are made from budget totals rather than being offset by function and subfunction and by agency.

Offsetting receipts are subdivided into two major categories:

Proprietary Receipts from the Public
Those collections from the public deposited in receipt accounts which arise from the conduct of business-type activities.

Intragovernmental Transactions
All collections or deposits into receipt accounts which the payment is made by a Federal agency. Intragovernmental transactions may represent either RECEIPTS FROM OFF-BUDGET FEDERAL ENTITIES, where a payment comes from a Federal entity whose funds are excluded from the budget totals, or INTRABUDGETARY TRANSACTIONS, where both the paying and the receiving accounts are within the budget. Intrabudgetary transactions in turn are further subdivided into three groups:

—Interfund transactions, where the payment is from a Federal to a trust fund or vice versa.
—Federal intrafund transactions, where both the paying and receiving accounts are Federal funds.
—Trust intrafund transactions, where both the paying and receiving accounts are trust funds.

ONE-YEAR AUTHORITY

See BUDGET AUTHORITY.

OPEN-ENDED PROGAMS

Entitlement programs under which actual obligations and resultant outlays are limited only by the number of eligible persons meeting eligibility requirements fixed by law who apply for benefits and the actual benefits received, e.g., medicaid.

OUTLAYS

The amount of checks issued, interest accrued on most public debt, or other payments; net of refunds and reimbursements. Total budget outlays consist of the sum of the outlays from appropriations and funds included in the unified budget, less offsetting receipts. The outlays of off-budget Federal entities are excluded from the unified budget under provisions of law, even though these outlays are part of total Government spending. Federal outlays are recorded on the "cash basis of accounting" — with the exception of most interest on the public debt, for which the "accrual basis of accounting" is used.

OVERSIGHT COMMITTEE

The congressional committee charged with general oversight of the operation of an agency or program. In some, but not all, cases the oversight committee for an agency also is the authorizing committee for that agency's programs. (See AUTHORIZING COMMITTEE.)

PAST YEAR

See FISCAL YEAR.

PERMANENT AUTHORITY

See BUDGET AUTHORITY.

PRESIDENT'S BUDGET

The budget for a particular fiscal year transmitted to the Congress by the President in accordance with the Budget and Accounting Act of 1921, as amended. Some elements of the budget, such as the estimates for the legislative branch and the judiciary, are required to be included without review by the Office of Management and Budget or approval by the President.

PROGRAM

Generally defined as an organized set of activities directed toward a common purpose, objective, or goal, undertaken or proposed by an agency in order to carry out responsibilities assigned to it. In practice, however, the term "program" has many usages and thus does not have a well-defined standardized meaning in the legislative process. "Program" has been used as a description for agency missions, "programs," activities, services, projects, and processes.

PROJECTIONS

Estimates of budget authority, outlays, receipts, or other budget amounts that extend several years into the future. Projections generally are intended to indicate the budgetary implications of continuing current or currently proposed programs and legislation for an indefinite period of time. These include alternative program and policy strategies and ranges of possible budget amounts. They generally should not be regarded as firm estimates of what actually will occur in future years nor as recommendations regarding future budget decisions.

PROPRIETARY RECEIPTS FROM THE PUBLIC

See OFFSETTING RECEIPTS.

PUBLIC DEBT

See FEDERAL DEBT.

PUBLIC ENTERPRISE REVOLVING FUND ACCOUNTS

See FEDERAL FUND ACCOUNTS.

REAPPORTIONMENT

A revision by the Office of Management and Budget of a previous apportionment of budgetary resources for an appropriation or fund account. A revision would ordinarily cover the same period, project, or activity covered in the original apportionment. (See APPORTIONMENT.)

REAPPROPRIATION

Congressional action to restore the obligational availability, whether for the same or different purposes, of all or part of the unobligated portion of budget authority in an expired account. Obligational availability in a current account may also be extended by a subsequent appropriation act.

RECEIPT ACCOUNTS

Accounts established for recording collections deposited into the Treasury for appropriation by the Congress. These accounts may be classified as general, special, or trust fund receipt accounts. (See FEDERAL FUND ACCOUNTS and TRUST FUNDS.)

RECEIPTS FROM OFF-BUDGET FEDERAL AGENCIES

See OFFSETTING RECEIPTS.

RECONCILIATION BILL

See RECONCILIATION PROCESS.

RECONCILIATION PROCESS

A process used by the Congress to reconcile amounts determined by tax, spending, and debt legislation for a given fiscal year with the ceilings enacted in the second required concurrent resolution on the budget for that year. Section 310 of the Congressional Budget Act of 1974 provides that the second required concurrent resolution on the budget, which sets binding totals for the budget, may direct committees to determine and recommend changes to laws, bills, and resolutions, as required to conform with the binding totals for budget authority, revenues, and the public debt. Such changes are incorporated into either a reconciliation resolution or a reconciliation bill.

Reconciliation Bill
A bill, requiring enactment by both Houses of the Congress and approval by the President, making changes to legislation that has been enacted or enrolled.

Reconciliation Resolution
A concurrent resolution, requiring passage by both Houses of Congress but not the approval of the President, directing the Clerk of the House or the Secretary of the Senate to make specified changes in bills or resolutions that have not yet reached the stage of enrollment.

RECONCILIATION RESOLUTION

See RECONCILIATION PROCESS.

REFUND

The return of an advance or the recovery of an erroneous disbursement from an appropriation or fund account that is directly related to, and a reduction of, previously recorded outlays from the account. It is also the return of excess collections deposited in receipt accounts that are treated as a reduction of receipts.

REIMBURSEMENTS

Sums received by the Government for commodities sold or services furnished either to the public or to another Government account that are authorized by law to be credited directly to specific appropriation and fund accounts. These amounts are deducted from the total obligations incurred (and outlays) in determining net obligations (and outlays) for such accounts.

REPROGRAMMING

Utilization of funds in an appropriation account for purposes other than those contemplated at the time of appropriation. Reprogramming is generally accomplished pursuant to consultation between the Federal agencies and the appropriate congressional committees.

RESCISSION

The consequence of enacted legislation which cancels budget authority previously provided by Congress prior to the time when the authority would otherwise lapse (i.e., cease to be available for obligation), Section 1012 of the Impoundment Control Act of 1974 requires a special message from the President to the Congress reporting any proposed rescission of budget authority. These proposals may be accepted in whole or in part through the passage of a rescission bill by both Houses of Congress.

RESCISSION BILL

A bill or joint resolution that provides for cancellation, in whole or in part, of budget authority previously granted by the Congress. Under the Impoundment Control Act of 1974, unless Congress approves a rescission bill within 45 days of continuous session after receipt of the proposal, the budget authority must be made available for obligation. (See RESCISSION.)

REVENUES

A term commonly used interchangeably with budget receipts. (See BUDGET RECEIPTS.)

REVOLVING FUND

A fund established to finance a cycle of operations through amounts received by the fund. There are three types of revolving funds: public enterprise, intragovernmental revolving, and trust revolving funds. (See also FEDERAL FUND ACCOUNTS and TRUST FUNDS.)

SCOREKEEPING

A procedure used by the Congressional Budget Office for up-to-date tabulations and reports of congressional budget actions on bills and resolutions providing new budget authority and outlays and changing revenues and the public debt limit for a fiscal year. Such reports shall include, but not be limited to, status reports on the effects of these congressional actions to date and of potential congressional actions, and comparisons of these actions to targets and ceilings set by Congress in the budget resolutions. Periodic scorekeeping reports are required by section 308(b) of the Congressional Budget Act of 1974.

SPECIAL FOREIGN CURRENCY PROGRAM APPROPRIATION

An appropriation made available to incur obligations for which payments must be made only in U.S.-owned foreign currencies that are declared in excess of the normal requirements of the United States by the Secretary of the Treasury. The appropriation is made in general fund dollar amounts which are credited to the account or fund generating the currency, or to miscellaneous receipts of the Treasury, as appropriate. The appropriated dollars are thereby exchanged for excess foreign currency (held in Treasury foreign currency fund accounts) that is used to make the necessary payments. (See also FOREIGN CURRENCY ACCOUNT.)

SPECIAL FUND ACCOUNTS

See FEDERAL FUND ACCOUNTS.

SPENDING AUTHORITY

As defined by the Congressional Budget Act of 1974, a collective designation for borrowing authority, contract authority, and entitlement authority, for which the budget authority is not provided in advance by appropriation acts. These are also commonly referred to as backdoor authority. (See BACKDOOR AUTHORITY.)

SPENDING COMMITTEES (SPENDING RESPONSIBILITY)

The standing committees of the House and Senate with jurisdiction over legislation that permits the obligations of funds. For most programs, the Appropriations Committees are the spending committees. For other programs, the authorizing legislation itself permits the obligation of funds (backdoor authority), in which case the authorizing committees are then the committees with spending responsibility.

SPENDING LEGISLATION (SPENDING BILL)

A term used in budget scorekeeping to indicate legislation that directly provides budget authority or outlays. The term includes (1) appropriations legislation, (2) legislation that provides budget authority directly without the need for subsequent appropriations action, and (3) entitlement legislation which, while requiring subsequent appropriations action, essentially "locks in" budget authority at the time of authorization (except legislation which establishes conditional entitlements, where recipients are entitled to payments only to the extent that funds are made available in subsequent appropriations legislation).

SUCCESSOR ACCOUNT

See "M" ACCOUNT.

SUPPLEMENTAL APPROPRIATION

An act appropriating funds in addition to those in an annual appropriation act. Supplemental appropriations provide additional budget authority beyond original estimates for programs or activities (including new programs authorized after the date of the original appropriation act) for which the need for funds is too urgent to be postponed until enactment of the next regular appropriation act.

TAX EXPENDITURES

Losses of tax revenue attributable to provisions of the Federal tax laws which allow a special exclusion, exemption, or deduction from gross income or which provide a special credit preferential rate of tax, or a deferral of tax liability.

TAX EXPENDITURES BUDGET

An enumeration of revenue losses resulting from "tax expenditures" under existing law for each fiscal year. Section 601 of the Congressional Budget Act of 1974 requires that estimated levels of tax expenditures be presented in the President's budget.

TOTAL OBLIGATIONAL AUTHORITY (TOA)

The sum of (1) all budget authority granted (or requested) from the Congress in a given year, (2) amounts authorized to be credited to a specific fund, and (3) unobligated balances of budget authority from previous years which remain available for obligation. In practice, this term is used primarily in discussing the Department of Defense budget but could be applied to other agencies' budgets as well.

TRANSFER APPROPRIATION ACCOUNT

A separate account established to receive and disburse allocations from another appropriation or fund account to carry out the purposes of the parent account or fund. The subsequent transactions of the transfer appropriation account are reported with the transactions of the parent account.

TRANSITION QUARTER (TQ)

The 3-month period (July 1 to September 30, 1976) between fiscal year 1976 and fiscal year 1977 resulting from the change from a July 1 through June 30 fiscal year to an October 1 through September 30 fiscal year beginning with fiscal year 1977.

TRUST FUNDS

Funds collected and used by the Federal Government for carrying out specific purposes and programs according to terms of a trust agreement or statute, such as the social security and unemployment trust funds. Trust funds are administered by the Government in a fiduciary capacity and are not available for the general purposes of the Government. Trust fund receipt accounts are credited with receipts generated by the terms of the trust agreement or statute. Trust fund receipts that are not anticipated to be used in the immediate future are generally invested in interest-bearing Government securities and earn interest for the trust fund. Trust fund expenditure accounts record amounts appropriated from trust fund receipts to be expended in carrying out the specific purposes or programs under the trust agreement or statute. A special category of trust funds called trust revolving funds, is used to carry out a cycle of business-type operations, e.g., the Federal Deposit Insurance Corporation.

TRUST INTRAFUND TRANSACTIONS

See OFFSETTING RECEIPTS.

TRUST REVOLVING FUNDS

See TRUST FUNDS and REVOLVING FUND.

UNDISTRIBUTED OFFSETTING RECEIPTS

See OFFSETTING RECEIPTS.

UNIFIED BUDGET

The present form of the budget of the Federal Government, in which receipts and outlays from Federal funds and trust funds are consolidated. When these fund groups are consolidated to display budget totals, transactions which are outlays of one fund group for payment to the other fund group (i.e., interfund transactions) are deducted to avoid double counting. Transactions of off-budget Federal entities are not included in the unified budget. (See OFFSETTING RECEIPTS and OFF-BUDGET FEDERAL ENTITIES.)

WARRANT

The official document issued pursuant to law

by the Secretary of the Treasury that establishes the amount of money authorized to be withdrawn from the Treasury.

ZERO-BASE BUDGETING

A budgeting technique that generally attempts to analyze budget requests without an implicit commitment to sustaining past levels of funding. Under this system programs and activities are organized and budgeted in a detailed plan that focuses review evaluation, and analysis on all proposed operations — rather than on increases above current levels of operations, as in incremental budgeting. Programs and activities are analyzed in terms of successively increasing levels of performance and funding, starting from zero, and then evaluated and ranked in priority order. The purpose is to determine the level, if any, at which each program or activity should be conducted.

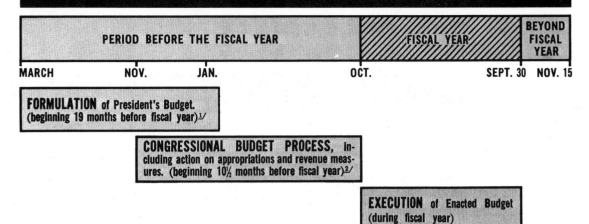

MAJOR STEPS IN THE BUDGET PROCESS

| PERIOD BEFORE THE FISCAL YEAR | FISCAL YEAR | BEYOND FISCAL YEAR |

MARCH   NOV.   JAN.   OCT.   SEPT. 30   NOV. 15

FORMULATION of President's Budget. (beginning 19 months before fiscal year)[1]

CONGRESSIONAL BUDGET PROCESS, including action on appropriations and revenue measures. (beginning 10½ months before fiscal year)[2]

EXECUTION of Enacted Budget (during fiscal year)

Final Data Available

[1] The President's budget is transmitted to Congress within fifteen days after Congress convenes.
[2] If appropriation action is not completed by Sept. 30, Congress enacts temporary appropriation (i.e., continuing resolution).

Source: Office of Management & Budget

FORMULATION OF PRESIDENT'S BUDGET

APPROXIMATE TIMING

	AGENCY	OFFICE OF MANAGEMENT AND BUDGET	THE PRESIDENT
BUDGET POLICY DEVELOPMENT		Develops economic assumptions. Obtains forecasts of international and domestic situations. Prepares fiscal projections.*	
MARCH (or earlier in some agencies)	Reviews current operations, program objectives, issues, and future plans in relation to upcoming annual budget. Submits projections of requirements that reflect current operations and future plans, supporting memoranda and related analytic studies that identify major issues, alternatives for resolving issues, and comparisons of costs and effectiveness.	Issues policy guidance on material to be developed for Spring planning review.	Discusses budgetary outlook and policies with the Director of the Office of Management and Budget, and with the Cabinet as appropriate.
APRIL **MAY**			
MAY		Discusses program developments and management issues, and resulting budgetary effects, with agencies.	
		Compiles total outlay estimates for comparison with revenue estimates. Develops recommendations for President on fiscal policy*, program issues, and budget levels.	Discusses with the Director of the Office of Management and Budget and others as necessary, general budget policy, major program issues, budgetary planning targets, and projections.
JUNE	Issues internal instructions on preparation of annual budget estimates.	Issues technical instructions for preparation of annual budget estimates.	Establishes general guidelines and agency planning targets for annual budget.
COMPILATION AND SUBMISSION OF AGENCY ESTIMATES		Conveys President's decisions to agency heads on Government-wide policies and assumptions, the application of policies, and budgetary planning targets to individual agencies.	
JULY– SEPTEMBER 30	Allocates budgetary planning target to agency programs. Develops and compiles detailed estimates.	Advises and assists agencies on preparation of budget submissions.	
OFFICE OF MANAGEMENT AND BUDGET REVIEW AND PRESIDENTIAL DECISIONS	Submits formal estimates for annual budget, including projections of requirements for future years and supporting materials.	Analyzes budget submissions. Holds hearings with agency representatives on program, budget, and management issues in preparation for Director's Review.	
SEPTEMBER **OCTOBER** **NOVEMBER**		Reexamines economic assumptions and fiscal policies.* Discusses program developments with agencies. In light of outlook and policy discussion with President, prepares budget recommendations for the President.	
	Revises estimates to conform to President's decisions.	Notifies agency heads of President's decisions.	Reviews budget recommendations and decides on agency budget amounts and on overall budget assumptions and policies.
DECEMBER **JANUARY** **FEBRUARY**		Again reviews economic outlook and fiscal policy for discussion with President of economic policies.*	Revises and approves budget message. Transmits recommended budget to Congress within 15 days after Congress convenes.
		Drafts President's budget message; prepares budget with summary tables, budget appendix, special analyses, and budget-in-brief. Arranges printing of budget documents.	

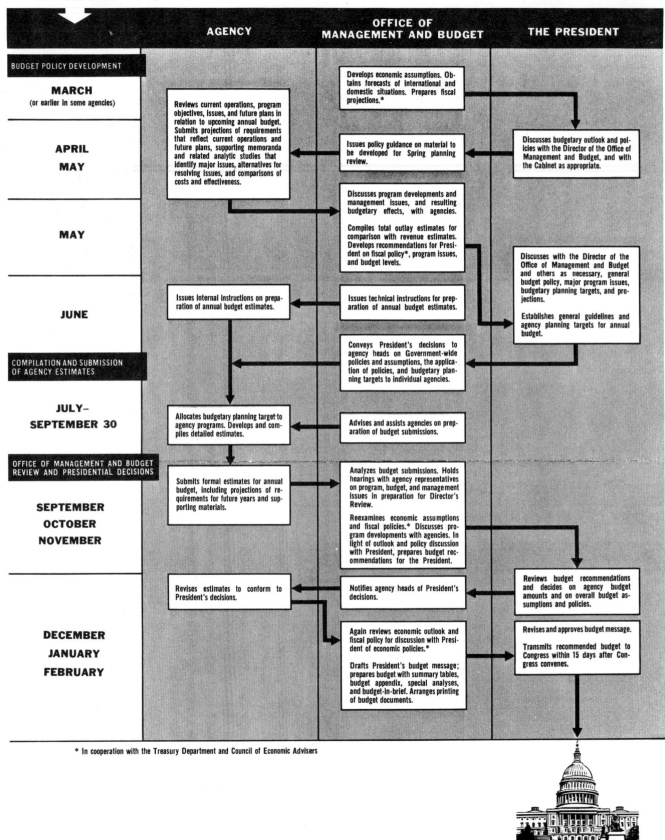

* In cooperation with the Treasury Department and Council of Economic Advisers

CONGRESSIONAL BUDGET PROCESS

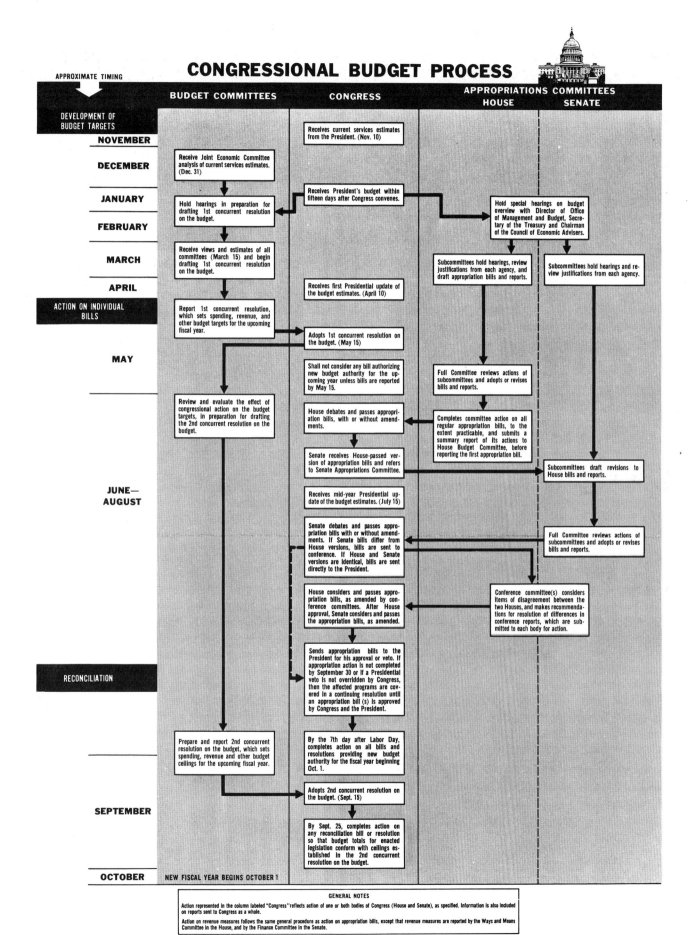

APPROXIMATE TIMING	BUDGET COMMITTEES	CONGRESS	APPROPRIATIONS COMMITTEES HOUSE	SENATE

DEVELOPMENT OF BUDGET TARGETS

NOVEMBER

Receives current services estimates from the President. (Nov. 10)

DECEMBER

Receive Joint Economic Committee analysis of current services estimates. (Dec. 31)

JANUARY

Receives President's budget within fifteen days after Congress convenes.

Hold hearings in preparation for drafting 1st concurrent resolution on the budget.

Hold special hearings on budget overview with Director of Office of Management and Budget, Secretary of the Treasury and Chairman of the Council of Economic Advisers.

FEBRUARY

MARCH

Receive views and estimates of all committees (March 15) and begin drafting 1st concurrent resolution on the budget.

Subcommittees hold hearings, review justifications from each agency, and draft appropriation bills and reports.

Subcommittees hold hearings and review justifications from each agency.

APRIL

Receives first Presidential update of the budget estimates. (April 10)

ACTION ON INDIVIDUAL BILLS

Report 1st concurrent resolution, which sets spending, revenue, and other budget targets for the upcoming fiscal year.

MAY

Adopts 1st concurrent resolution on the budget. (May 15)

Shall not consider any bill authorizing new budget authority for the upcoming year unless bills are reported by May 15.

Full Committee reviews actions of subcommittees and adopts or revises bills and reports.

Review and evaluate the effect of congressional action on the budget targets, in preparation for drafting the 2nd concurrent resolution on the budget.

House debates and passes appropriation bills, with or without amendments.

Completes committee action on all regular appropriation bills, to the extent practicable, and submits a summary report of its actions to House Budget Committee, before reporting the first appropriation bill.

Senate receives House-passed version of appropriation bills and refers to Senate Appropriations Committee.

Subcommittees draft revisions to House bills and reports.

JUNE— AUGUST

Receives mid-year Presidential update of the budget estimates. (July 15)

Senate debates and passes appropriation bills with or without amendments. If Senate bills differ from House versions, bills are sent to conference. If House and Senate versions are identical, bills are sent directly to the President.

Full Committee reviews actions of subcommittees and adopts or revises bills and reports.

House considers and passes appropriation bills, as amended by conference committees. After House approval, Senate considers and passes the appropriation bills, as amended.

Conference committee(s) considers items of disagreement between the two Houses, and makes recommendations for resolution of differences in conference reports, which are submitted to each body for action.

RECONCILIATION

Sends appropriation bills to the President for his approval or veto. If appropriation action is not completed by September 30 or if a Presidential veto is not overridden by Congress, then the affected programs are covered in a continuing resolution until an appropriation bill (s) is approved by Congress and the President.

Prepare and report 2nd concurrent resolution on the budget, which sets spending, revenue and other budget ceilings for the upcoming fiscal year.

By the 7th day after Labor Day, completes action on all bills and resolutions providing new budget authority for the fiscal year beginning Oct. 1.

Adopts 2nd concurrent resolution on the budget. (Sept. 15)

SEPTEMBER

By Sept. 25, completes action on any reconciliation bill or resolution so that budget totals for enacted legislation conform with ceilings established in the 2nd concurrent resolution on the budget.

OCTOBER NEW FISCAL YEAR BEGINS OCTOBER 1

GENERAL NOTES

Action represented in the column labeled "Congress" reflects action of one or both bodies of Congress (House and Senate), as specified. Information is also included on reports sent to Congress as a whole.

Action on revenue measures follows the same general procedure as action on appropriation bills, except that revenue measures are reported by the Ways and Means Committee in the House, and by the Finance Committee in the Senate.

EXECUTION OF ENACTED BUDGET

TREASURY-GEN. ACCOUNTING OFFICE	AGENCY	OFFICE OF MANAGEMENT AND BUDGET
On approval of appropriation bill, appropriation warrant is drawn by Treasury and is forwarded to agency.	Revenues are assessed, collected, and deposited by the agencies concerned as prescribed by law.	

FUNDS MADE AVAILABLE
AUG.–SEPT.

	Revises operating budget in view of approved appropriations and program developments. Prepares requests for apportionment by Aug. 21 or within 10 days after approval of appropriations, whichever is later.	
		Makes apportionment by Sept. 10 or within 30 days after approval of appropriations, whichever is later. May reapportion at any time, on own initiative or on agency request. May withhold funds through the apportionment process as a deferral or as an amount withheld pending rescission. Such withholding requires transmittal by the President of special messages to the Congress for its approval or disapproval.

CONTROL OVER FUNDS
Continuous

	Allots apportioned funds to various programs or activities. Restricts obligations through administrative controls to apportioned and allotted amounts. Obligates money. Receives and uses goods and services. Makes monthly or quarterly reports to Office of Management and Budget on status of funds and use of resources in relation to program plans. Reports periodically to Office of Management and Budget on management improvements and actions affecting personnel requirements and costs.	
		Examines reports on status of funds in relation to apportionments. Analyzes reports on use of resources and relationship of accomplishments and costs. Reports to the President from time to time on budget and program status, personnel, management improvements, and cost reductions.

EXPENDITURE OF FUNDS
As bills become payable

	Prepares and certifies vouchers and invoices for payment.	
Treasury issues checks (except for certain agencies which issue their own) and reports on financial transactions in Monthly Treasury Statement, Treasury Bulletin, and Combined Statement of Receipts, Expenditures and Balances of the United States Government.		

PROGRAM EVALUATION, MANAGEMENT APPRAISAL, AND INDEPENDENT AUDIT
Periodic

General Accounting Office performs independent audit of financial records, transactions, and financial management, generally. "Settles" accounts of certifying and disbursing officers. Makes reports to Congress including reports on special messages on deferrals and proposed rescissions.	Reviews compliance with established policies, procedures, and requirements. Evaluates accomplishment of program plans and effectiveness of management and operations.	Reviews agency operations and evaluates programs and performance. Conducts or guides agencies in organization and management studies. Assists President in improving management and organization of the Executive Branch.

PART III
PUBLICATION: HOW TO FIND U.S. STATUTES AND U.S. CODE CITATIONS

One of the important steps in the enactment of a valid law is the requirement that it shall be made known to the people who are to be bound by it. In practice, our laws are published immediately upon their enactment so that they may be known to the people.

If the President approves a bill, or allows it to become law without his signature, the original enrolled bill is sent from the White House to the Administrator of General Services for publication. If a bill is passed by both Houses over the objections of the President, the body that last overrides the veto likewise transmits it. There it is assigned a public law number, and paginated for the Statutes at Large volume covering that session of the Congress. The public and private law numbers run in sequence starting anew at the beginning of each Congress, and since 1957 are prefixed for ready identification by the number of the Congress — e.g., the first public law of the 97th Congress (1981-1982) is designated Public Law 97-1 and the first private law of the 97th Congress is designated Private Law 97-1. Subsequent laws of this Congress also will contain the same prefix designator.

"SLIP LAWS"

The first official publication of the statute is in the form generally known as the "slip law." (See below page 77). In this form, each law is published separately as an unbound pamphlet. Slip laws are printed by photoelectric offset process from the original enrolled bill. This process ensures accuracy and saves both time and expense in preparing the copy. The heading indicates the public or private law number, the date of approval, and the bill number. Beginning in 1976, the heading of a slip law for a public law also indicates the United States Statutes at Large citation. If the statute has been passed over the veto of the President, or has become law without his signature because he did not return it with his objections, an appropriate statement is inserted in lieu of the usual notation of approval.

The Office of the Federal Register (General Services Administration) which prepares the slip laws, provides marginal editorial notes giving the citations to laws mentioned in the text and other explanatory details. Beginning in 1974, the marginal notes also give the United States Code classifications, thus enabling the reader immediately to determine where the statute will appear in the Code. Beginning in 1975, each slip law also includes an informative guide to the legislative history of the law consisting of the committee report number, the name of the committee in each House, as well as the date of consideration and passage in each House, with reference to the *Congressional Record* by volume, year, and date. Since 1971, a reference to Presidential statements — relating to the approval of a bill (or the veto of a bill when the veto was overridden and the bill becomes law) — has been included in the legislative history in the form of a citation to the Weekly Compilation of Presidential Documents.

Copies of the slip laws are delivered to the document rooms of both Houses where they become available to officials and the public. They may also be obtained by annual subscription or individual purchase from the Government Printing Office.

STATUTES AT LARGE

For the purpose of providing a permanent collection of the laws of each session of the Congress, the bound volumes, which are called the United States Statutes at Large, are prepared by the General Services Administration. Each volume contains a complete index and a table of contents. From 1956 through 1975, each volume contained a table of earlier laws affected. From 1963 through 1974, each volume also contained a most useful table showing the legislative history of each law in the volume. This latter table was not included in subsequent volumes because, beginning in 1975, the legislative histories have appeared at the end of each law. There are also extensive marginal notes referring to laws in earlier volumes and to earlier and later matters in the same volume.

The Statutes at Large are a chronological arrangement of the laws exactly as they have been enacted. There is no attempt here to arrange the laws according to their subject matter or to show the present status of an earlier law that has been amended. That is the function of the United States Code.

UNITED STATES CODE

The United States Code contains a consolidation and codification of the general and permanent laws of the United States arranged according to subject matter under fifty title headings. It sets out the current status of the laws, as amended, without repeating all the language of the amendatory acts except where necessary for that purpose. Its purpose is to present the laws in a concise and usable form without requiring recourse to the many volumes of the Statutes at Large containing the individual amendments.

The Code is prepared by the Law Revision Counsel of the House of Representatives. New editions are published every six years and cumulative supplements are published after the conclusion of each regular session of the Congress.

HOW TO FIND CITATIONS TO U.S. STATUTES AT LARGE AND U.S. CODE

The "How to Find" guide that follows is designed to enable the reader to obtain — quickly and easily — an up-to-date and accurate citation of the U.S. Statutes at Large and the U.S. Code. Part IV below will offer a guide to the use of the *Federal Register*.

In using the research procedure chart,* beginning on page 78, the reader should read the items from left to right across the two pages.

The *first* column contains the typical references which require further citing, which are (1) Revised Statutes section, (2) date of law, (3) name of law, (4) number of law, (5) Statutes citation, and (6) Code citation; the *second, third,* and *fourth* columns point to the official published volumes in which the citations may be found and suggest logical sequences to follow in making the search; *column five* suggests additional finding aids, some of which especially are useful for citing current legislation; and the *last* column shows some examples of the citations resulting from following the steps in the chart.

The careful following of the steps set forth carries the assurance that each search will be complete and that all appropriate points will have been covered.

Publications referred to in abbreviated form are identified and described in a convenient list on pages 84 and 85.

---

*The chart presented here is extracted from the Office of Federal Register pamphlet entitled "How to Find U.S. Statutes and U.S. Code Citations," published by the Government Printing Office.

PRINCIPAL FINDING AIDS*

Slip Law

U.S. Statutes at Large

U.S. Code

**U.S. Code
Supplement**

---

*For description see "REFERENCES" on pages 84 and 85.

RESEARCH PROCEDURE CHART

IF YOU HAVE this reference—	AND YOU USE THESE basic finding aids—	
	U.S. STATUTES AT LARGE (new volume added each year)	U.S. CODE [1] (new edition every 6 years)
1. Revised Statutes Section.......... [e.g., Rev. Stat. 56]	[Revised Statutes, 1873, were published as pt. 1, vol. 18, U.S. Statutes at Large; 2d edition published in 1878.]	Use tables in U.S.C. Popular Names and Tables volume to find U.S.C. section; verify text; then—
2. Date of Laws: [2] *(a)* For any year *up to* and *through* year of last edition of U.S.C. [e.g., June 22, 1942];	Use Stat. volume for that year to check the List of Public Laws; get law number and verify page number from List; then—	Use tables in U.S.C. Popular Names and Tables volume to find U.S.C. section; verify text; then—
(b) For any year *after* year of last edition of U.S.C. and *through* year of latest Supplement;	Use Stat. volume for that year to check the List of Public Laws; get law number and verify page number from List; then—	....
(c) For current year........................	....	....
3. Name of Law: *(a)* For any year *up to* and *through* year of last edition of U.S.C. [e.g., Government in the Sunshine Act];	....	Use Acts Cited by Popular Name index (in U.S.C. Popular Names and Tables volume) to obtain Stat. and U.S.C. citations; verify both; then—
(b) For any year *after* year of last edition of U.S.C. and *through* year of latest Supplement [e.g., Airline Deregulation Act of 1978];	....	....
(c) For current year........................	....	....

See footnote at end of table, p. 82.

PLUS latest published— U.S. CODE SUPPLEMENT (*all* changes since last edition)	AND/OR THESE additional finding aids— (See "REFERENCES," p. 84)	YOU SHOULD GET this citation—
Check latest U.S.C. Supplement for recent changes; verify text.	Check Table 3 in latest U.S.C. Cong. & Adm. News for changes during current period; if Code section is included, verify text in same publication or in slip law.	Rev. Stat. 56. 2 U.S.C. 64.
Check latest U.S.C. Supplement for recent changes; verify text.	Check Table 3 in latest U.S.C. Cong. & Adm. News for changes during current period; if Code section is included, verify text in same publication or in slip law.	56 Stat. 377. 36 U.S.C. 171–178.
Use tables in latest U.S.C. Supplement to find U.S.C. section; verify text.	Check Table 3 in latest U.S.C. Cong. & Adm. News for changes during current period; if Code section is included, verify text in same publication or in slip law.	
	Use slip law or U.S.C. Cong. & Adm. News *text* to get law number, Stat. citation, and to verify subject matter; also use Table 2, U.S.C. Cong. & Adm. News to find U.S.C. classification.	
Check latest U.S.C. Supplement for recent changes; verify text.		90 Stat. 1241. 5 U.S.C. 552b note.
Use Acts Cited by Popular Name index (preceding Tables in U.S.C. Supplement) to obtain Stat. and U.S.C. citation; verify both; then—	Check Table 3 in latest U.S.C. Cong. & Adm. News for changes during current period; verify any changes in same publication or in slip law. Other sources: Index of Popular Name Acts Affected in U.S. Statutes at Large *Laws Affected Tables, 1956–70 and 1971–75;* Table of Federal Statutes by Popular Names in U.S. Supreme Court Reports; Shepard's Acts and Cases by Popular Name; U.S.C.A. Popular Name Table; U.S.C.S. tables volume.	92 Stat. 1705. 49 U.S.C. 1301 note.
	Use House Calendar *index* and *numerical list* to get bill number, then law number (if assigned); or U.S.C. Cong. & Adm. News *index* or Table 10; use slip law or U.S.C. Cong. & Adm. News *text* to get Stat. citation and U.S.C. classification, and to verify date and subject matter; also, with law number, use Table 2, U.S.C. Cong. & Adm. News, to find U.S.C. classification.	

RESEARCH PROCEDURE CHART—Continued

IF YOU HAVE this reference—	AND YOU SEE THESE basic finding aids—	
	U.S. STATUTES AT LARGE (new volume added each year)	U.S. CODE [1] (new edition every 6 years)
4. Number of Law:		
(a) For any year *up to* and *through* year of last edition of U.S.C. and the law—		
(1) *does not* have a numerical prefix [e.g., Public Law 702];	[You will need additional information, such as the Congress, the year, or the Stat. volume—year 1956 used here; then] use the Stat. volume to check the List of Public Laws; get and verify page number from List; then—	Use tables in U.S.C. Popular Names and Tables volume to find U.S.C. section; verify text; then—
(2) *does* have a numerical prefix [e.g., Public Law 94–369];	Use Stat. volume for the Congress indicated by the numerical prefix; check the List of Public Laws; get and verify page number from List; then—	Use tables in U.S.C. Popular Names and Tables volume to find U.S.C. section; verify text; then—
(b) For any year *after* last edition of U.S.C. and *through* year of latest Supplement [e.g., Public Law 95–521];	Use Stat. volume for the Congress indicated by the numerical prefix; check the List of Public Laws; get and verify page number from List; then—	....
(c) For current year [e.g., Public Law 96–223].	....	....
5. Stat. Citation: [3]		
(a) For any year *up to* and *through* year of last edition of U.S.C. [e.g., 90 Stat. 1255];	Use Stat. volume to get date and law number; verify subject matter, then—	Use tables in U.S.C. Popular Names and Tables volume to find U.S.C. section; verify text; then—
(b) For any year *after* year of last edition of U.S.C. and *through* year of latest Supplement [e.g., 91 Stat. 685];	Use Stat. volume to get date and law number; verify subject matter, then—	....
(c) For current year	....	....

See footnote at end of table, p. 82.

PLUS latest published— U.S. CODE SUPPLEMENT (*all* changes since last edition)	AND/OR THESE additional finding aids— (See "REFERENCES," p. 84)	YOU SHOULD GET this citation—
Check latest U.S.C. Supplement for recent changes; verify text.	Check Table 3 in latest U.S.C. Cong. & Adm. News for changes during current period; if Code section is included, verify text in same publication or in slip law.	70 Stat. 531. 25 U.S.C. 304a.
Check latest U.S.C. Supplement for recent changes; verify text.	Check Table 3 in latest U.S.C. Cong. & Adm. News for changes during current period; if Code section is included, verify text in same publication or in slip law.	90 Stat. 999. 42 U.S.C. 6701 *et seq.*
Use tables in latest U.S.C. Supplement to find U.S.C. section; verify text.	Check Table 3 in latest U.S.C. Cong. & Adm. News for changes during current period; if Code section is included, verify text in same publication or in slip law.	92 Stat. 1824. 2 U.S.C. 701 *et seq.*
....	Use slip law or U.S.C. Cong. & Adm. News *text* to get Stat. citation, U.S.C. classification, and to verify date and subject matter; also, with law number, use Table 2, U.S.C. Cong. & Adm. News to find U.S.C. classification.	94 Stat. 229. 26 U.S.C. 1 note.
Check latest U.S.C. Supplement for recent changes; verify text; then—	Check Table 3 in latest U.S.C. Cong. & Adm. News for changes during current period; if Code section is included, verify text in same publication or in slip law.	90 Stat. 1255. 50 U.S.C. 1601 *et seq.*
Use tables in latest U.S.C. Supplement to find U.S.C. section; verify text; then—	Check Table 3 in latest U.S.C. Cong. & Adm. News for changes during current period; if Code section is included, verify text in same publication or in slip law.	91 Stat. 685. 42 U.S.C. 7401 *et seq.*
....	Use slip law or U.S.C. Cong. & Adm. News *text* to verify subject matter, date, U.S.C. classification and law number. Table 2, U.S.C. Cong. & Adm. News also may be used to find U.S.C. classification.	

RESEARCH PROCEDURE CHART—Continued

IF YOU HAVE this reference—	AND YOU USE THESE basic finding aids—	
	U.S. STATUTES AT LARGE (new volume added each year)	U.S. CODE [1] (new edition every 6 years)
6. U.S.C. Citation: (a) For any year *up to* and *through* year of last edition of U.S.C. [e.g., 17 U.S.C. 102]:	....	Check section in U.S.C. to verify subject matter and determine appropriate Stat. citation; verify text against Stat. volume; then—
(b) For any year *after* year of last edition of U.S.C. and *through* year of latest Supplement [e.g., 20 U.S.C. 3401];	....	....
(c) For current year...............	....	....

[1] If U.S. Code is not available, use U.S.C.A. or U.S.C.S. and their supplements.
[2] You will need some knowledge of the subject matter if more than one law was signed on the same day.
[3] You will need some knowledge of the subject matter if more than one law appears on the same page.

PLUS latest published— U.S. CODE SUPPLEMENT (*all* changes since last edition)	AND/OR THESE additional finding aids— (See "REFERENCES," p. 84)	YOU SHOULD GET this citation—
Check latest U.S.C. Supplement for recent changes; verify text; then—	Check Table 3 in latest U.S.C. Cong. & Adm. News for changes during current period; if Code section is included, verify text in same publication or in slip law.	90 Stat. 2544. 17 U.S.C. 102.
Check section in latest U.S.C. Supplement to verify subject matter and determine appropriate Stat. citation; verify text against Stat. volume; then—	Check Table 3 in latest U.S.C. Cong. & Adm. News for changes during current period; if Code section is included, verify text in same publication or in slip law.	93 Stat. 669. 20 U.S.C. 3401.
....	Check Table 3 in latest U.S.C. Cong. & Adm. News; if Code section is included, get page number on which text of law appears and get law number from that page (Code citation should appear as a marginal note), then verify Stat. citation and subject matter from slip law.	

REFERENCES

Title	Description
Government Publications:	
A. Principal Finding Aids	
1. Slip law	A pamphlet print of each public and private law enacted by Congress, issued a few days after a bill becomes law; public (but not private) slip laws carry the Statutes page numbers that will be their permanent citation in a future Statutes volume, marginal notes and citations (including U.S. Code and D.C. Code classifications of current legislation), and a guide to legislative history (which also contains dates of related Presidential statements); text of both public and private laws with annotations are later cumulated and bound as part of the Stat. volume.
2. Stat	United States Statutes at Large; contains all public and private laws and concurrent resolutions enacted during a session of Congress, plus reorganization plans, proposed and ratified amendments to the Constitution, and proclamations by the President, with finding aids including legislative history, subject index, and Laws Affected Tables (see item 5 below); arrangement is chronological by approval date in each category; by law, these volumes are "legal evidence" (1 U.S.C. 112); only the general and permanent laws are codified (arranged by subject in titles) in the U.S.C.
3. U.S.C	United States Code and its annual, cumulative supplements; published every six years; only the general and permanent laws of the United States are codified (arranged by subject in titles) in the U.S. Code; temporary, local, or private laws are not included; the Code establishes "prima facie the laws of the United States" except "whenever titles of such Code shall have been enacted into positive law the text thereof shall be legal evidence" (1 U.S.C. 204(a)); to date, 20 titles and subtitle IV of Title 49 have been enacted into positive law; contains list of Acts by popular name, index and tables.
4. U.S.C. Supplement	Annual, cumulative supplements to the United States Code; contains all changes in or additions to the general and permanent laws and Code ancillaries since the last edition of the Code.
B. Others	
5. Laws Affected Tables ...	Published in each Statutes volume, from 1956 through 1976, showing the prior laws affected by the public laws in each volume; after 1976 Statutes volume, the Tables were discontinued, and are no longer prepared.
6. Laws Affected Tables for 1956–1970 and 1971–1975.	15-year cumulation and 5-year cumulation, published separately; contains Index of Popular Name Acts Affected; cumulations are no longer prepared and were discontinued after the 1971–1975 cumulation.
7. House Calendar	Calendars of the U.S. House of Representatives and History of Legislation (1 publication)—very useful for following day-to-day progress of legislation through both Houses of Congress; index, usually on Mondays; final edition covers the session (1st) or the Congress (end of 2d session).
8. Index Analysis of the Federal Statutes, 1789–1873; Index to the Federal Statutes, 1874–1931.	Subject index covering all general and permanent laws through 46 Stat. (Mar. 4, 1931); useful for tracing early legislation.

Title	Description
Non-Government Publications:	
9. U.S.C. Cong. and Adm. News.	United States Code Congressional and Administrative News— published at least monthly during each session of Congress; monthly when Congress is not in session. Gives slip law information, including legislative history; has subject index, list of popular name acts, tables; material is currently supplemental to and annually codified in U.S.C.A.
10. U.S.C.A. and supplements.	United States Code Annotated—an annotated version of the U.S. Code with periodic supplements and annual, cumulative pocket parts.
11. U.S.C.S. and supplements.	United States Code Service—annotated version of U.S. Code with monthly advance service containing text of slip laws, proclamations, etc., and cumulative tables and index; annual, cumulative pocket parts.
12. Shepard's Acts and Cases by Popular Name.	Bound volume of Federal and State Acts by popular name or short title with U.S. Code and U.S. Statutes at Large citations; cumulative supplements.

O

PART IV
THE FEDERAL REGISTER AND ITS USE

INTRODUCTION

The previous three parts traced the Federal legislative process, from the introduction of a bill to its enactment into law. This legislation is, in most cases, implemented by Federal agencies as rules and regulations, which are published as part of the Federal Register System.*

The Federal Register System is comprised primarily of two major publications, the daily **Federal Register (FR)** and the annually revised **Code of Federal Regulations (CFR).** The two publications work together to provide an up-to-date version of regulations promulgated by the Federal agencies.

A basic function of the Federal Register System is to allow for citizen participation in the regulatory process. This is in recognition of the fact that regulatory activity of the Federal agencies has increased dramatically in recent years, in volume, complexity, and impact on individual members of the public. It is important for the individual to understand the system and how to participate in it. In the material that follows, we will attempt a basic introduction to the Federal Register System, using a number of illustrations.

The last part of this section includes Government telephone numbers to call for additional information on the **Federal Register** and **Code of Federal Regulations.**

The steps in the codification (i.e., official publishing) of legislation and regulations is given in the charts beginning on the next page.

---

*The material presented in this part has been extracted in part from the publication, *The Federal Register: What It Is and How to Use It.*, published by the Government Printing Office. For a more detailed discussion on the subject, consult that publication.

Parallel Codification of Legislation and Regulations

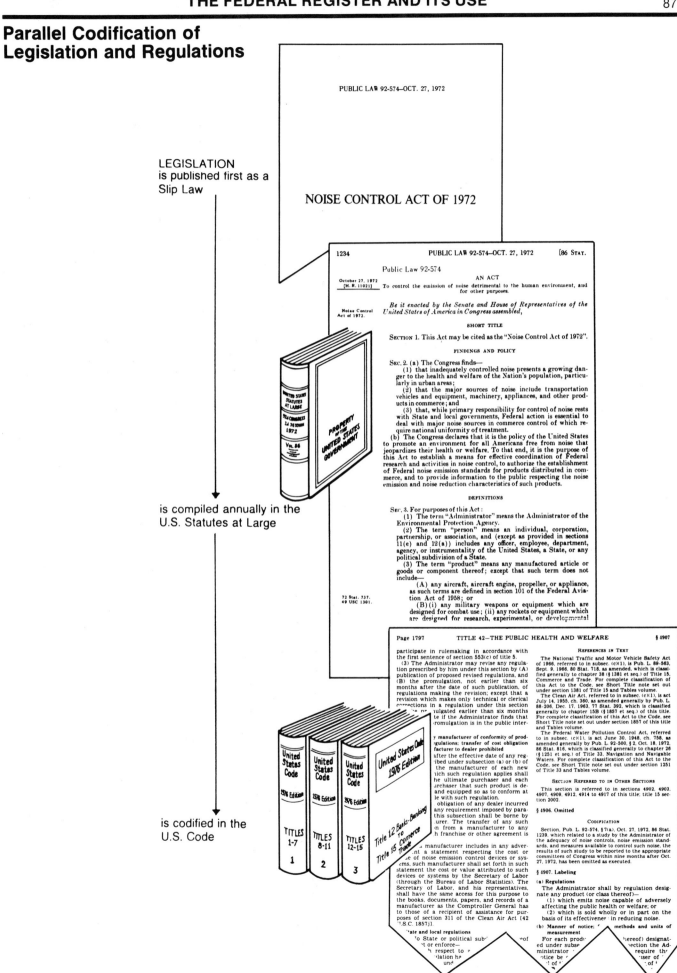

PUBLIC LAW 92-574—OCT. 27, 1972

LEGISLATION
is published first as a
Slip Law

NOISE CONTROL ACT OF 1972

1234   PUBLIC LAW 92-574—OCT. 27, 1972   [86 Stat.

Public Law 92-574

October 27, 1972   AN ACT
[H. R. 11021]   To control the emission of noise detrimental to the human environment, and
                   for other purposes.

Noise Control   Be it enacted by the Senate and House of Representatives of the
Act of 1972.   United States of America in Congress assembled,

                              SHORT TITLE

        Section 1. This Act may be cited as the "Noise Control Act of 1972".

                           FINDINGS AND POLICY

        Sec. 2. (a) The Congress finds—
            (1) that inadequately controlled noise presents a growing dan-
        ger to the health and welfare of the Nation's population, particu-
        larly in urban areas;
            (2) that the major sources of noise include transportation
        vehicles and equipment, machinery, appliances, and other prod-
        ucts in commerce; and
            (3) that, while primary responsibility for control of noise rests
        with State and local governments, Federal action is essential to
        deal with major noise sources in commerce control of which re-
        quire national uniformity of treatment.
        (b) The Congress declares that it is the policy of the United States
        to promote an environment for all Americans free from noise that
        jeopardizes their health or welfare. To that end, it is the purpose of
        this Act to establish a means for effective coordination of Federal
        research and activities in noise control, to authorize the establishment
        of Federal noise emission standards for products distributed in com-
        merce, and to provide information to the public respecting the noise
        emission and noise reduction characteristics of such products.

                              DEFINITIONS

        Sec. 3. For purposes of this Act:
            (1) The term "Administrator" means the Administrator of the
        Environmental Protection Agency.
            (2) The term "person" means an individual, corporation,
        partnership, or association, and (except as provided in sections
        11(e) and 12(a)) includes any officer, employee, department,
        agency, or instrumentality of the United States, a State, or any
        political subdivision of a State.
            (3) The term "product" means any manufactured article or
        goods or component thereof; except that such term does not
        include—
72 Stat. 737.   (A) any aircraft, aircraft engine, propeller, or appliance,
49 USC 1301.   as such terms are defined in section 101 of the Federal Avia-
                   tion Act of 1958; or
                       (B)(i) any military weapons or equipment which are
                   designed for combat use; (ii) any rockets or equipment which
                   are designed for research, experimental, or developmental

is compiled annually in the
U.S. Statutes at Large

is codified in the
U.S. Code

Page 1797   TITLE 42—THE PUBLIC HEALTH AND WELFARE   § 4907

participate in rulemaking in accordance with   REFERENCES IN TEXT
the first sentence of section 553(c) of title 5.   The National Traffic and Motor Vehicle Safety Act
    (3) The Administrator may revise any regula-   of 1966. referred to in subsec. (c)(1), is Pub. L. 89-563,
tion prescribed by him under this section by (A)   Sept. 9. 1966. 80 Stat. 718, as amended, which is classi-
publication of proposed revised regulations, and   fied generally to chapter 38 (§ 1381 et seq.) of Title 15.
(B) the promulgation, not earlier than six   Commerce and Trade. For complete classification of
months after the date of such publication, of   this Act to the Code, see Short Title note set out
regulations making the revision; except that a   under section 1381 of Title 15 and Tables volume.
revision which makes only technical or clerical   The Clean Air Act. referred to in subsec. (c)(1), is act
corrections in a regulation under this section   July 14. 1955. ch. 360. as amended generally by Pub. L.
        ....ulgated earlier than six months 88-206. Dec. 17. 1963. 77 Stat. 392, which is classified
....te if the Administrator finds that   generally to chapter 15B (§ 1857 et seq.) of this title.
.......romulgation is in the public inter-   For complete classification of this Act to the Code, see
                                                    Short Title note set out under section 1857 of this title
....y manufacturer of conformity of prod-   and Tables volume.
....gulations; transfer of cost obligation   The Federal Water Pollution Control Act, referred
....facturer to dealer prohibited   to in subsec. (c)(1). is act June 30. 1948. ch. 758, as
        ..... after the effective date of any reg- amended generally by Pub. L. 92-500. § 2. Oct. 18. 1972.
....ibed under subsection (a) or (b) of   86 Stat. 816, which is classified generally to chapter 26
.... the manufacturer of each new   (§ 1251 et seq.) of Title 33, Navigation and Navigable
....nich such regulation applies shall   Waters. For complete classification of this Act to the
....he ultimate purchaser and each   Code, see Short Title note set out under section 1251
....urchaser that such product is de-   of Title 33 and Tables volume.
....and equipped so as to conform at
....le with such regulation.   SECTION REFERRED TO IN OTHER SECTIONS
    ... obligation of any dealer incurred   This section is referred to in sections 4902, 4903,
.... this subsection shall be borne by   4907. 4909. 4912. 4914 to 4917 of this title; title 15 sec-
....urer. The transfer of any such   tion 2002.
....n from a manufacturer to any
....h franchise or other agreement is   § 4906. Omitted

.... manufacturer includes in any adver-   CODIFICATION
    ...nt a statement respecting the cost or   Section, Pub. L. 92-574. § 7(a). Oct. 27. 1972. 86 Stat.
    ...ue of noise emission control devices or sys- 1239. which related to a study by the Administrator of
....ems, such manufacturer shall set forth in such the adequacy of noise controls. noise emission stand-
statement the cost or value attributed to such   ards, and measures available to control such noise. the
devices or systems by the Secretary of Labor   results of such study to be reported to the appropriate
(through the Bureau of Labor Statistics). The   committees of Congress within nine months after Oct.
Secretary of Labor, and his representatives.   27. 1972. has been omitted as executed.
shall have the same access for this purpose to
the books, documents, papers, and records of a   § 4907. Labeling
manufacturer as the Comptroller General has
to those of a recipient of assistance for pur-   (a) Regulations
poses of section 311 of the Clean Air Act (42   The Administrator shall by regulation desig-
U.S.C. 1857j].   nate any product (or class thereof)—
    ....ate and local regulations   (1) which emits noise capable of adversely
        .....o State or political sub-.... ....of   affecting the public health or welfare; or
    ....t or enforce—   (2) which is sold wholly or in part on the
        ....h respect to ....   basis of its effectivenes in reducing noise.
        ....lation ha...   (b) Manner of notice;   methods and units of
        .... und ....   measurement
                                                       For each prod...   ....hereof) designated
                                                    ....ed under subse...   ....ction the Ad-
                                                    ....ministrator ....require th
                                                    ....tice be ....iser of
                                                    ....t of ....of

REGULATIONS
appear as
agency documents

which are published
daily in the
Federal Register

and codified annually in the
Code of Federal Regulations

---

79 30067

ENVIRONMENTAL PROTECTION AGENCY

40 CFR PART 211

[FRL 1270-2]

APPROVAL AND PROMULGATION OF THE

GENERAL PROVISIONS FOR

PRODUCT NOISE LABELING

AGENCY: U.S. Environmental Protection Agency (EPA)

ACTION: Final Rule

SUMMARY: By this notice the Environmental Protection Agency establishes the general provisions of a regulatory program for product

---

31722   PROPOSED RULES

ENVIRONMENTAL PROTECTION AGENCY

[40 CFR Part 211]

[FRL 722-8]

NOISE LABELING STANDARDS
General Provisions

AGENCY: Environmental Protection Agency.

ACTION: Notice of proposed rulemaking.

SUMMARY: By this notice the Environmental Protection Agency...

for individual products or product classes will be added to these provisions by future rulemaking actions. The major purpose of the regulatory action being proposed is to provide accurate and understandable information to product purchasers and users concerning the noise generating or noise reducing properties of products so that meaningful comparisons can be made by the public concerning such properties as part of purchase or use decisions.

FOR FURTHER INFORMATION CONTACT:
Ms. Ellen Robinson, Public Information Specialist, U.S. Environmental Protection Agency, Office of Public Affairs (A-107), 401 M Street, SW., Washington, D.C. 20460, 202-755-0704.

SUPPLEMENTARY INFORMATION: See following text

By this notice the Environmental Protection Agency proposes to establish the

---

56120   Federal Register / Vol. 44, No. 190 / Friday, September 28, 1979 / Rules and Regulations

ENVIRONMENTAL PROTECTION AGENCY

40 CFR Part 211

[FRL 1270-2]

Approval and Promulgation of the General Provisions for Product Noise Labeling

AGENCY: U.S. Environmental Protection Agency (EPA).

ACTION: Final rule.

SUMMARY: By this notice the Environmental Protection Agency establishes the general provisions of a regulatory program for product noise labeling under the authority of Section 8 of the Noise Control Act of 1972. 42 U.S.C. 4907. These general provisions concern the aspects of the program which the Agency intends to apply in every instance of product noise labeling. The practicality of applying the general provisions will be determined for each product to be noise labeled. The Agency will address the labeling requirements for individual products or product classes, which differ with these provisions, in product-specific rulemaking actions. The major purpose of this regulatory program is to provide accurate and understandable information on the noise reducing properties of products. so that the meaningful comparisons of those properties when deciding to use or buy the product.

EFFECTIVE DATE: Sept...

FOR FURTHER INFORM...
Timothy McBride, St...
Regulation Division (...
Environmental Prote...
Washington, D.C. 20...

SUPPLEMENTARY INFO...

I. Introduction

On June 22, 1977, th... Protection Agency (F... proposed rule (42 FR... a product noise label... the authority of, and... Section 8 of the Nois... 1972. 42 U.S.C. 4907... proposal set forth the... of the noise labeling... and established Part... the Code of Federal...

211 will be composed of the general labeling provisions as subpart A, and individual product-specific labeling requirements that would be added as further subparts by separate rulemaking actions. Because of a computerization program undertaken since the promulgation of the proposed rule, it was necessary in the final rule to either replace the second decimal point in each section heading with a zero or delete it entirely. At the time of publication, the EPA solicited written public comment on the proposed General Provisions as well as all other aspects of the proposed product noise labeling program. Public hearings were not initially scheduled. The public comment period for the proposed rule was originally set at 90 days with closing scheduled for September 20, 1977. As the result of receiving a large number of letters shortly after publication in the Federal Register, the EPA decided to schedule public hearings on the proposed rule and extended the comment period to October 28, 1977 (42 FR 41139). Hearings were held in Washington, D.C. on September 16, 1977; in Cedar Rapids, Iowa on September 20, 1977; and in San Francisco, California on September 22, 1977.

In all, the Agency received 735 written comments by the close of the comment period. and took oral testimony from 51

general provisions and product-specific regulations must be considered in tandem; and that, therefore, issuing the general provisions before the product-specific regulations serves no useful purpose. Commenters wanted to be certain that they could comment on the General Provisions and also be able to comment on product-specific regulations, if the Agency proposed product regulations affecting their industry. One commenter indicated that comments on the General Provisions should be considered in future product-specific rulemaking. That same commenter also stated that there were enormous problems in selecting a label format and what sort of relevant information should be included on the product(s) to be regulated. Another commenter argued that the proposed standards would create confusion and procedural dilemmas when they were applied to a particular product, since they apply neither to a specific product nor to all products in general.

The EPA proposed the noise labeling General Provisions at the same time it proposed a product-specific noise labeling regulation for Hearing Protectors (42 FR 31730). Thus, the General Provisions do not exist alone. The Agency believes that the one-time issuance of the Product Noise Labeling

---

code of federal regulations

40

Protection of Environment

PARTS 100 TO 399

Revised as of July 1, 1980

Organization of the Federal Register/Code of Federal Regulations System

The Federal Register System is comprised primarily of two major publications, the daily *Federal Register* (*FR*) and the annually revised *Code of Federal Regulations* (*CFR*). The two publications work together to provide an up-to-date version of any agency regulation. To understand the system, one needs to understand each separate publication as well as the relationship between the two publications.

Code of Federal Regulations (CFR)

The *Code of Federal Regulations (CFR)* is an annually revised codification of the general and permanent rules published in the *Federal Register* by the executive departments and agencies of the Federal Government. The *CFR* is divided into 50 titles which represent broad areas subject to Federal regulation.

List of CFR Titles [Revised as of December 1979]

1. General Provisions	19. Customs Duties	35. Panama Canal
2. [Reserved]	20. Employees' Benefits	36. Parks, Forests, and Public Property
3. The President	21. Food and Drugs	
4. Accounts	22. Foreign Relations	37. Patents, Trademarks, and Copyrights
5. Administrative Personnel	23. Highways	
6. Economic Stabilization	24. Housing and Urban Development	38. Pensions, Bonuses and Veterans' Relief
7. Agriculture		
8. Aliens and Nationality	25. Indians	39. Postal Service
9. Animals and Animal Products	26. Internal Revenue	40. Protection of Environment
10. Energy	27. Alcohol, Tobacco Products and Firearms	41. Public Contracts and Property Management
11. Federal Elections		
12. Banks and Banking	28. Judicial Administration	42. Public Health
13. Business Credit and Assistance	29. Labor	43. Public Lands: Interior
	30. Mineral Resources	44. Emergency Management and Assistance
14. Aeronautics and Space	31. Money and Finance: Treasury	
15. Commerce and Foreign Trade		45. Public Welfare
16. Commercial Practices	32. National Defense	46. Shipping
17. Commodity and Securities Exchanges	32A. National Defense, Appendix	47. Telecommunication
	33. Navigation and Navigable Waters	48. [Reserved]*
18. Conservation of Power and Water Resources		49. Transportation
	34. Education	50. Wildlife and Fisheries

*Reserved for Federal Acquisition Regulations

Each volume of the *CFR* is revised at least once each calendar year and issued on a quarterly basis approximately as follows:

Title 1 through Title 16	as of January 1
Title 17 through Title 27	as of April 1
Title 28 through Title 41	as of July 1
Title 42 through Title 50	as of October 1

The appropriate revision date is printed on the cover of each volume. Each year's cover is a different color for quick reference.

The full text of the *CFR* contains amendments published in the *Federal Register* since the last revision of the volume of the *CFR*. If no amendments were published during the revision period for an individual volume, a cover will be issued indicating that the prior year's edition is current and should be retained.

The regulations in Title 37 are contained in one volume.

The regulations in Title 18 are contained in two volumes, one of which contains Parts 0 to 149 and the other, Parts 150 to end.

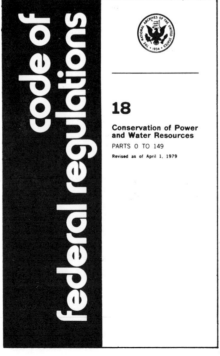
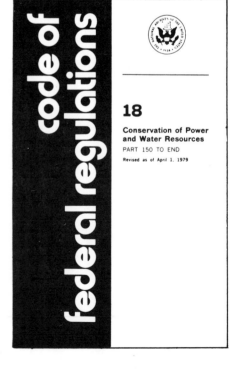

The 50 titles of the *CFR* represent broad areas subject to regulatory action. Each title is broken down into chapters, which usually bear the name of the issuing agency; chapters are divided into parts covering specific regulatory areas; parts are divided into sections, the basic unit of the *CFR*; and if further breakdown is necessary it is to the paragraph level.

Basic numbering

Example of basic numbering.
Title 8—Aliens and Nationality
Chapter I—Immigration and Naturalization Service, Department of Justice
Part 235—Inspection of Persons Applying for Admission
Section 235.10—U.S. Citizen Identification Card
    (a) *General*
    (b) *Eligibility*
    (c) *Application*

Title

Title. Each title represents a broad area that is subject to Federal regulation—e.g., Title 7 deals with agriculture, Title 29 with labor, Title 46 with shipping. Subtitles, lettered consecutively in capitals (A, B, C, etc.), are sometimes used to distinguish between the regulations of an overall agency and its various bureaus. Subtitles are also used to group related chapters.

Chapter

Chapter. Each chapter is numbered in Roman capitals (I, II, III, etc.) and usually is assigned to a single issuing agency, which may be an entire department or one of its units. Chapters are sometimes divided into subchapters, lettered in capitals (A, B, C, etc.) to group related parts. Title 41 is an exception—the chapters are in Arabic numbers. Each Title 41 volume contains an explanation of its numbering system.

Part

Part. Each chapter is divided into parts, numbered in Arabic throughout each title (1, 2, 3, etc.). A part consists of a unified body of regulations applying to a single function of the issuing agency or devoted to a specific subject matter under control of the issuing agency. Subparts, lettered in capitals, sometimes are used to group related sections within a part.

Section

Section. Each section number includes the number of the part set off by a period preceded by the symbol "§." For example, the third section in Part 25 is expressed as "§ 25.3."

The section is the basic unit of the *CFR* and ideally consists of a short, simple presentation of one proposition.

Paragraph

Paragraph. When internal division of a section is necessary, sections are divided into paragraphs. Paragraphs may be further subdivided as follows:

Term	Symbol
Paragraph	(a), (b), (c), etc.
For further subdividing of a paragraph	(1), (2), (3), etc.
	(i), (ii), (iii), etc.
	(A), (B), (C), etc.*
	(*1*), (*2*), (*3*), etc.
	(*i*), (*ii*), (*iii*), etc.

*Italic lower case letters are frequently used for this particular category.

The Table of Contents for the chapter leads directly to each part.

CHAPTER I—DEPARTMENT OF STATE

The Table of Contents for each part lists part numbers on the left, separated from section numbers on the right by a period.

§ 3a.7   **Title 22—Foreign Relations**

by the Secretary concerned or his designee.

§ 3a.7 Notification of disapproval and reconsideration.

(a) The Director, Bureau of Politico-Military Affairs, will notify the applicant directly when an applicant's proposed foreign employment is disapproved, and will inform the Secretary concerned.

(b) Each notification of disapproval under this section must include a statement of the reasons for the disapproval, with as much specificity as security and foreign policy considerations permit, together with a notice of the applicant's right to seek reconsideration of the disapproval under paragraph (c) of this section.

(c) Within 60 days after receipt of the notice of disapproval, an applicant whose request has been disapproved may submit a request for reconsideration by the Director, Bureau of Politico-Military Affairs. A request for reconsideration should provide information relevant to the reasons set forth in the notice of disapproval.

(d) The disapproval of a request by the Director, Bureau of Politico-Military Affairs, will be final, unless a timely request for reconsideration is received. In the event of a request for reconsideration, the Director, Bureau of Politico-Military Affairs, will make a final decision after reviewing the record of the request. A final decision after reconsideration to approve the applicant's proposed employment with a foreign government will be communicated to the Secretary concerned as provided in § 3a.6. A final decision after reconsideration to disapprove applicant's proposed employment foreign government 'll be d dir oli f

ally changed, either by a substantial change in duties from those described in the request upon which the original approval was based, or by a change of employer, the applicant must obtain further approval in accordance with this part for such changed employment.

PART 4—NOTIFICATION OF FOREIGN OFFICIAL STATUS

Sec.
4.1 Persons required to give notification.
4.2 Persons exempted from the requirement to give notification.
4.3 Form to be used in giving notification.
4.4 Form required in duplicate.
4.5 Time limit for the submission of the form.
4.6 Termination of official status and departure from the United States.

AUTHORITY: Sec. 10, 56 Stat. 257, sec. 4, 63 Stat. 111, as amended; 22 U.S.C. 620, 2658.

SOURCE: 22 FR 10788, Dec. 27, 1957, unless otherwise noted.

§ 4.1 Persons required to give notification.

All persons who are entitled to exemption from the registration and fingerprinting requirements of the Alien Registration Act of 1940 (54 Stat. 670), as amended, are required to give notification to the Secretary of State of their presence in the United States. Such persons comprise foreign government officials, members of their families (including relatives by blood or marriage regularly residing in or forming a part of their household), and their employees and attendants.

§ 4.2 Persons exempted from the requirement to give notification.

Ambassadors and ministers, and members of their missio^ ^amed in the ^^matic List iss^ ^ by ^ment o^

The authority citation following the Table of Contents is provided, and kept current, by the agency. It gives the legislative (or Statutory), or occasionally Presidential or agency, authority under which a part, or section within a part, is issued.

The source note is supplied by the Office of the Federal Register. It tells where the codified material was last published in the *Federal Register* in full, by volume, page, and date. The source note for the entire part follows the authority citation; if a section is added or amended later, its source note would follow the text of that section.

Following the codified text each *CFR* book contains a number of "finding aids," which will be described below.

CFR Index and finding aids

The *CFR Index and finding aids* is a separate volume of the *CFR*. It is revised semiannually, as of January 1 and July 1. It comes as part of a subscription to the *CFR* or can be purchased as an individual volume.

The basic part of the book consists of an index arranged by agency names and broad subject headings covering rules currently codified in the *CFR*, keyed to each title and part. It is necessarily a very broad approach due to its coverage of over 83,000 pages.

There are four auxiliary finding aids included:
- (1) List of agency-prepared indexes appearing in individual *CFR* volumes;
- (2) Parallel table of authorities and rules (a three-part listing designed to lead the user from legislation to regulation);
- (3) Acts requiring publication in the *Federal Register;* and
- (4) List of CFR Titles, Chapters, Subchapters, and Parts.

These are in addition to the alphabetical list of agencies appearing in the *CFR*, which is contained in every *CFR* volume.

Samples are shown on the following pages. Each listing is self-explanatory.

code of federal regulations

CFR Index
and finding aids
Revised as of July 1, 1979

CFR Index

National Aeronautics

Interior Department, interagency motor
vehicle pools, 41 CFR 114–39
Interior Department, motor equipment
management, 41 CFR 114–38
Insurance cost information availability
from automobile dealers, 49 CFR 582

Lease and interchange of vehicles, 49
CFR

Manufactu
26 CF

National n
maxin
CFR

National p
CFR

Odometer
CFR

Operators.

Sale of ret
access
1956,

Seizure an
and a
aliens

Seizure an
and a
count
securi
401

Stolen pro
with

Tire adver
CFR

Wake Isla

Moving c

Freight fo
shipp
Tariffs
Motor car
sched
1307
Transpc
co

Munition

See Arms

Museums
Museum services program, 45 CFR 64

Music
Air Force bands, 32 CFR 820

Army Department, bands, competition
with civilian bands, 32 CFR 508

LIST OF AGENCY-PREPARED INDEXES APPEARING IN INDIVIDUAL CFR VOLUMES

Code of Federal Regulations Title and chapter or part	Agency
1 CFR Chapter I	Administrative Committee of the Federal Register
3 CFR	The President
7 CFR Part 2852	Food Safety and Quality Service
11 CFR Parts 100–115	Federal Election Commission
14 CFR	
19 CFR	
21 CFR	
23 CFR	
29 CFR	
32 CFR	
35 CFR	
37 CFR	
43 CFR	
46 CFR	
49 CFR	

TABLE I—PARALLEL TABLE OF AUTHORITIES AND RULES

The following table lists all sections of the United States Code (except 5 U.S.C. 301), and the United States Statutes at Large which are cited as rule-making authority for currently effective rules codified in the Code of Federal Regulations, or which are noted as being interpreted or applied by those rules. The table is arrange
by the
include
Execut

1 U. S. C. 3   **CFR Index**

United States Code	Code of Federal Regulations
1 U. S. C. 3	46 CFR Part 66
2 U. S. C. 136	36 CFR Parts 701–703
437d	11 CFR Parts 100–115
	Parts 120–125
	Parts 140–146
	Part 9031
438	11 CFR Parts 100–115
451	14 CFR Part 374a
	47 CFR Part 64
3 U. S. C. 202	31 CFR Part 409
301	32 CFR Part 719
	Part 762

Table I—Authorities
35 Stat. 450

United States Statutes at Large	Code of Federal Regulations
26 Stat. 712	25 CFR Part 124
31 Stat. 1449	15 CFR Parts 7–7b
32 Stat. 390	43 CFR Part 419
792	9 CFR Part 72
33 Stat. 1265	9 CFR Part 72
34 Stat. 539	25 CFR Part 74
	Part 177
543	25 CFR Part 175
	Part 183

PARALLEL TABLE OF STATUTORY AUTHORITIES AND RULES

Proclamations:

April 28, 1916	25 Part 88
658	36 Part 7
2028	43 Part 3820
2039	43 Part 3820
2228	36 Part 12
2232	43 Part 3820
2351	
2544	
2554	
3004	
3279	
3339	
3447	
4040	
4138	
4313	
4547	
4611	

Executi

4601	
5389	
5464	
6073	
6166	
6260	
6560	
6614	
6910	
2	
2	
6964	
2	
2	
7786	
7964	
8143	
8389	
8428	
8785	

Directives:

May 17, 1972	14 Part 1203
	29 Part 14

Memorandums:

May 21, 1956	32 Part 240
May 21, 1963	14 Part

TABLE III—ACTS REQUIRING PUBLICATION IN THE FEDERAL REGISTER

The Federal Register Act (44 U.S.C. 1501–1515) and the Administrative Procedure Act (5 U.S.C. 551–559) are the basic acts requiring or authorizing the publication of documents in the FEDERAL REGISTER. This appendix lists the acts contemplated by section 5(a)(3) of the Federal Register Act and hence requiring or authorizing such publication.

This Table III should be distinguished from the parallel table of statutory authori-

Contents—Title 1

List of CFR Titles, Chapters, Subchapters, and Parts

(Revised as of July 1, 1979)

TITLE 1—GENERAL PROVISIONS

Chapter I—Administrative Committee of the Federal Register (Parts 0--49)

SUBCHAPTER A—GENERAL

Part
1   Definitions.
2   General information.
3   Services to the public.

Federal Register (FR)

The *Federal Register (FR)* is a serial publication which contains documents in the following categories:

Presidential Documents, Rules and Regulations, Proposed Rules, Notices, and Sunshine Act Meetings. Often documents are published as separate parts of the *FR* following the main body of the issue to allow the issuing agencies to order reprints. Each *FR* also includes various "finding aids" which are research tools prepared by the Office of the Federal Register (OFR).

There is an addition of the *FR* for each official Federal working day. The *FR* is the vehicle that keeps the *CFR* up-to-date.

Federal Register Documents

Briefly described, the different categories are as follows:
(1) Presidential Documents—documents signed by the President and submitted to the Office of the Federal Register (OFR) for publication;
(2) Rules and Regulations—regulatory documents having general applicability and legal effect;
(3) Proposed Rules—notices to the public of the proposed issuance of rules and regulations;
(4) Notices—documents other than rules and proposed rules that are applicable to the public; and
(5) Sunshine Act Meetings—notices of meetings published under the Government in the Sunshine Act (5 U.S.C. 552b(e)(3)).

The preferred citation for *FR* material is by volume and page number, both of which are printed at the top of each page. For example, the final rule shown on page 101 would be 44 *FR* 55332.

On the following pages are examples of each of the five types of documents appearing in the *FR*.

Cover. On the cover of each day's issue of the *FR* are its date, volume, number, and inclusive page numbers. If the material is contained in more than one book, this information is given for the extra book(s) as well.

There are also the beginning entries of the Highlights listing, which are selective special interest subjects. The Highlights continues inside.

12-10-79
Vol. 44—No. 238

BOOK 1:
PAGES
70701-71100

12-10-79
Vol. 44—No. 238
BOOK 2:
PAGES
71101-71398

Book 1 of 2 Books
Monday, December 10, 1979

Highlights

CONTINUED INSIDE

Rules and Regulations

Rules and Regulations. The Rules and Regulations section contains regulatory documents having general applicability and legal effect, most of which are keyed to and codified in the *CFR*. The terms "rules" and "regulations" have the same meaning for publication purposes.

Each document begins with a heading which includes the name of the issuing agency (and subagency if appropriate), the *CFR* title and part(s) affected, and a brief description of the contents. In some cases agencies include a document number for use in their own internal document retrieval system.

Preamble

Following the heading is the preamble, which (since April 1, 1977) must accompany the regulatory text of all proposed or final rulemaking documents. The preamble requirements (published in full in 1 CFR 18.12) are intended to improve the clarity of documents published in the *FR*. The preamble must be in the following format and contain the specified information:

AGENCY: ————————————
(Name of issuing agency)

ACTION: ————————————
(Notice of Intent), (Advance Notice of Proposed Rulemaking), (Proposed Rule), (Final Rule), (Other).

SUMMARY: ————————————
(Brief statements, in simple language, of: (i) the action being taken; (ii) the circumstances which created the need for the action; and (iii) the intended effect of the action.)

DATES: ————————————
(Comments must be received on or before: ————.) (Proposed effective date: ————.) (Effective date: ————.) (Hearing: ————.) (Other: ————.)

ADDRESSES: ————————————
(Any relevant addresses.)

FOR FURTHER INFORMATION CONTACT: ————————————
————————————
(For Executive departments and agencies, the name and telephone number of a person in the agency to contact for additional information about the document.)

SUPPLEMENTARY INFORMATION: ——
————————————
As required by the provisions of paragraph (c) of 1 CFR 18.12.

55332 Federal Register / Vol. 44, No. 188 / Wednesday, September 26, 1979 / Rules and Regulations

DEPARTMENT OF JUSTICE

Drug Enforcement Administration

21 CFR Part 1316

Administrative Hearings; Amendment of Hearing Procedures

AGENCY: Drug Enforcement Administration, United States Department of Justice.

ACTION: Final rule.

SUMMARY: This rule amends the DEA hearing procedures to provide for the filing of exceptions to the findings of fact, conclusions of law and decision recommended or proposed by the Administrative Law Judge, prior to certification of the record to the Administrator.

EFFECTIVE DATE: September 26, 1979.

FOR FURTHER INFORMATION CONTACT: Stephen E. Stone, Attorney, Office of the Chief Counsel, Drug Enforcement Administration, Washington, D.C. 20537. Telephone (202) 633-1141.

SUPPLEMENTARY INFORMATION: By Final Rule dated July 13, 1979, published in the **Federal Register**, 44 FR 42178, on July 19, 1979, the Administrator of the Drug Enforcement Administration established a procedure for the filing of exceptions to the decision, findings of fact and conclusions of law proposed or recommended by the Administrative Law Judge. This procedure provided that a twenty day period for filing such exceptions would commence to run on the date upon which a party was served with a copy of the Administrative Law Judge's report to the Administrator. In practice, this occurred simultaneously with certification of the record to the Administrator. This procedure has proven to be inefficient and confusing. In order to remedy this situation, the Administrator has decided to further modify the procedures to provide for the filing of exceptions prior to the certification of the record to the Administrator.

Therefore, under the authority vested in him by the Controlled Substances Act and the regulations of the Department of Justice, the Administrator of the Drug Enforcement Administration hereby orders that Part 1316 of Title 21, Code of Federal Regulations, be amended as follows:

1. Section 1316.65 (b) and (c) are amended to read:

§ 1316.65   Report and record.

*   *   *   *   *

(b) The presiding officer shall serve a copy of his report upon each party in the hearing. The report shall be considered to have been served when it is mailed to such party or its attorney of record.

(c) Not less than twenty-five days after the date on which he caused copies of his report to be served upon the parties, the presiding officer shall certify to the Administrator the record, which shall contain the transcript of testimony, exhibits, the findings of fact and conclusions of law proposed by the parties, the presiding officer's report, and any exceptions thereto which may have been filed by the parties.

2. Section 1316.66 is amended to read:

§ 1316.66   Exceptions.

(a) Within twenty days after the date upon which a party is served a copy of the report of the presiding officer, such party may file with the Hearing Clerk, Office of the Administrative Law Judge, exceptions to the recommended decision, findings of fact and conclusions of law contained in the report. The party shall include a statement of supporting reasons for such exceptions, together with evidence of record (including specific and complete citations of the pages of the transcript and exhibits) and citations of the authorities relied upon.

(b) The Hearing Clerk shall cause such filings to become part of the record of the proceeding.

(c) The Administrative Law Judge may, upon the request of any party to a proceeding, grant time beyond the twenty days provided in paragraph (a) of this section for the filing of a response to the exceptions filed by another party, if he determines that no party in the hearing will be unduly prejudiced and that the ends of justice will be served thereby. Provided, however, that each party shall be entitled to only one filing under this section; that is, either a set of exceptions or a response thereto.

3. The first sentence of § 1316.67 is amended to read:

§ 1316.67   Final order.

As soon as practicable after the presiding officer has certified the record to the Administrator, the Administrator shall cause to be published in the **Federal Register** his final order in the proceeding, which shall set forth the final rule and the findings of fact and conclusions of law upon which the rule is based. * * *

Dated: September 20, 1979.

Peter B. Bensinger,
Administrator.

[FR Doc. 79-29856 Filed 9-25-79; 8:45 am]
BILLING CODE 4110-09-M

The illustration here is of a final rule promulgated by the Justice Department. Other documents classified as Rules and Regulations are interim rules, temporary regulations, and notices of deferral.

Proposed Rules

Proposed Rules. Proposed rules are notices to the public of the proposed issuance of rules and regulations. Publication of proposed rules gives interested persons the opportunity to participate in the rulemaking process prior to the adoption of final rules.

The format and preamble requirements for documents in the Proposed Rules section are the same as for final rules. Within the preamble the date given is generally the deadline for submission of comments. (Since Executive Order 12044 of March 24, 1978 (43 FR 12661) the comment period has been set at at least 60 days for significant proposed rules; if this is not feasible, an explanation must accompany the proposed rule.) An address paragraph is also included for submission of comments.

Most proposed rules are documents that suggest amendments to agency regulations in the *CFR* and request public comment on those suggested changes. The majority of proposed rules are required to be published as such by section 553 of the Administrative Procedure Act or other statutory authority. Additionally, many agencies voluntarily publish amendments, exempted from notice and comment requirements, in proposed form to allow public comment.

Federal Register / Vol. 44, No. 215 / Monday, November 5, 1979 / Proposed Rules   63753

FEDERAL ELECTION COMMISSION

11 CFR Part 9033

[Notice 1979-19]

Presidential Primary Matching Fund

AGENCY: Federal Election Commission.

ACTION: Notice of proposed rulemaking.

SUMMARY: The Commission requests comments on proposed rules to govern the administration of the Presidential Primary Matching Fund Account provided for in Chapter 96 of Title 26 United States Code. The revisions of the regulations at 11 CFR Chapter I concern the suspension of matching fund payments to candidates who exceed the expenditure limitations at 11 CFR 9035. The proposed revision would eliminate the current procedure permitting resumption of payments to such a candidate.

DATES: Comments must be received on or before December 5, 1979.

ADDRESSES: Address comments to Patricia Ann Fiori, Assistant General Counsel, Federal Election Commission, 1325 K Street, N.W., Washington, D.C. 20463.

FOR FURTHER INFORMATION CONTACT: Patricia Ann Fiori, Assistant General Counsel (202) 523-4143.

SUPPLEMENTARY INFORMATION: Current regulations provide that if the Commission determines that a publicly financed candidate has knowingly and willfully exceeded expenditure limitations, matching fund payments to that candidate will be suspended.

Current regulations also provide that a candidate whose payments have been suspended may become entitled to resumption of payments upon repayment of an amount equal to the excessive expenditure and payment or agreement to pay any civil or criminal penalties resulting from the violation. The proposed revisions would permit the Commission to suspend payments to a candidate who knowingly, willfully *and substantially* exceeds expenditure limitations. Moreover, such a candidate would be prohibited from receiving any further payments.

PART 9033—ELIGIBILITY

11 CFR 9033.8 is revised to read as follows:

§ 9033.8 Suspension of Payments.

(a) If the Commission has reason to believe that a candidate has knowingly, willfully and substantially failed to comply with the disclosure requirements of 2 USC 434 and 11 CFR Part 104, or that a candidate has knowingly, willfully and substantially exceeded the expenditure limitations at 11 CFR 9035, the Commission may make an initial determination to suspend payments to that candidate.

(b) The Commission shall notify the candidate of its initial determination, giving the legal and factual reasons for the determination and advising the candidate of the evidence upon which its initial determination is based. The candidate shall be given an opportunity within 20 days of the Commission's notice to comply with the above cited

provisions or to submit written legal or factual materials to demonstrate that he or she is not in violation of those provisions.

(c) The Commission shall consider any written legal or factual materials submitted by the candidate in making its final determination. Such materials may be submitted by counsel if the candidate so desires.

(d) A final determination to suspend payments by the Commission shall be accompanied by a written statement of reasons for the Commission's action. This statement shall explain the reasons underlying the Commission's determination and shall summarize the results of any investigation upon which the determination is based.

(e)(1) A candidate whose payments have been suspended for failure to comply with reporting requirements may become entitled to receive payments if he or she complies with reporting requirements and pays or agrees to pay any civil or criminal penalties resulting from failure to comply.

(2) A candidate whose payments were suspended for exceeding expenditure limitations shall not be entitled to receive further matching payments under 11 CFR 9034.1.

Dated: October 30, 1979.

Robert O. Tiernan,
Chairman, Federal Election Commission.

[FR Doc. 79-34145 Filed 11-2-79; 8:45 am]

BILLING CODE 6715-01-M

One of the earliest steps in the rulemaking process is the petition for rulemaking. The agency document in response to the petition, classified in the Proposed Rules section because the petition proposes to amend, add to, or delete specific portions of the *CFR*, requests public comment. Not every agency employs the concept of "petitions" for rulemaking.

52076   Federal Register / Vol. 44, No. 174 / Thursday, September 6, 1979 / Proposed Rules

DEPARTMENT OF TRANSPORTATION

Federal Aviation Administration

[14 CFR Ch. I]

[Docket No. 18691; Notice No. PR-79-9]

Petition for Rulemaking of the Air Transport Association of America, Airport Noise Abatement Plans: Regulatory Process

AGENCY: Federal Aviation Administration (FAA), DOT.

ACTION: Publication of petition for rule making; request for comments.

SUMMARY: This notice publishes for public comment the petition and supporting documents of the Air Transport Association of America (ATA), dated January 16, 1979, on behalf of its member air carriers, for amendment of the Federal Aviation Regulations to add a new Part 150 (14 CFR Part 150) to those provisions applicable to airports. The ATA petition requests, for the reasons disclosed, the Administrator to initiate rule-making proceedings to adopt regulations prescribing the process under which airport noise abatement plans, or similar restrictions upon the operation of aircraft at an FAA certificated airport, must be submitted to and considered by the FAA before the plan is implemented or enforced.

The ATA's petition involves some issues that are similar to those involved in a notice of proposed rule making issued by the FAA in 1976 based on recommended regulations submitted to it by the U.S. Environmental Protection Agency under section 611(c) of the Federal Aviation Act of 1958, as amended. That notice (Notice No. 76–24), among other things, contains proposals to require development and submission of airport noise abatement plans and periodic up-dates to those plans by all proprietors of civil airports certificated by the FAA under Part 139. Those proposals, if adopted, would prescribe the regulatory process for development, approval, and implementation of airport noise abatement plans which would be approved by the F~ ~ ~art

differences, as well as the similarities, between the two regulatory approaches to airport noise abatement plans; and (2) to ensure due consideration of each separately under the applicable FAA rule-making procedures. Although this notice sets forth without change the contents of the ATA petition as received by the FAA, its publication in accordance with FAA procedures governing the processing of petitions for rule making does not represent an FAA position on the merits of the petition. Unlike Notice No. 74–22, which contained the EPA's recommended regulations, this notice does not propose any amendment of the current rules. If, after consideration of the available data and comments received in response to this notice, the FAA determines it should initiate rule-making proceedings based on the ATA petition, a notice of proposed rule making containing specific regulatory proposals will be issued.

DATES: Comments must be received on or before November 5, 1979.

ADDRESSES: Send comments on the petition in duplicate to: Federal Aviation Administration, Office of the Chief Counsel, Attn: Rules Docket (AGC–24), Docket N. 18691, 800 Independence Avenue, SW., Washington, D.C. 20591.

FOR FURTHER INFORMATION CONTACT: Richard Tedrick, Noise Policy and Regulations Branch (AEE–110), Noise Abatement Division, Office of Environment and Energy, Federal Aviation Administration, 800 Independence Avenue, SW., Washington, D.C. 20591; telephone (202) 755–9027.

SUPPLEMENTARY INFORMATION:

I. Comments Invited

Interested persons are invited to submit such written data, views, or arguments on the petition for rule making as they may desire. Communications should identify the docket or petition notice number and be submitted in duplicate to the address indicated above. All communications timely received will be considered by the FAA before taking action on the petition for rule making. All comments submitted will be available for examination in the Rules Docket.

The ATA Petition

Accordingly, the Federal Aviation Administration publishes verbatim for public comment the following petition for rule making of the Air Transport Association of America, dated January 16, 1979.

Issued in Washington, D.C., on August 30, 1979.

Edward P. Faberman,
Acting Assistant Chief Counsel, Regulations & Enforcement Division.

Air Transport Association of America, *1709 New York Avenue, N.W., Washington, D.C. January 16, 1979.*

Hon. Langhorne M. Bond, *Administrator, Federal Aviation Administration, Washington, D.C.*

Re: A Regulatory Proposal, Petition for Rulemaking—Airport Noise Abatement Plans.

Dear Mr. Bond: Pursuant to the procedural rules of the Federal Aviation Administration (FAA), the Air Transport Association of America (ATA) on behalf of its member airlines hereby files the attached petition to the Administrator for the issuance of a notice of proposed rulemaking to adopt a regulation governing the promulgation of airport noise abatement plans.

★ ★ ★ ★ ★ ★ ★

Docket

Petition For Rule-Making Air Transport Association of America, Airport Noise Abatement Plans

Petition for Rule-Making

Pursuant to § 11.25 of the Procedural Rules of the Federal Aviation Administration (FAA), the Air Transport Association of America (ATA) on behalf of its member airlines hereby petitions the Administrator to institute a rule-making proceeding to promulgate a regulation which provides that any airport noise abatement plan, or similar restriction upon the operation of an FAA certificated airport, must be submitted to the Administrator of the FAA for review. In support of its petition, ATA respectfully states as follows:

★ ★ ★ ★ ★ ★ ★

★ ★ ★ ★ ★ ★ ★

Another preliminary document to a proposal, but carried in the Proposed Rule section, is the advance notice of proposed rulemaking, or the notice of intent. Agencies issue these documents at an early stage in the rulemaking process to receive public reaction as early as possible. The documents describe a problem or situation and the anticipated regulatory action of the agency. They seek public response concerning the necessity for regulating in the area and the adequacy of the agency's anticipated regulatory response. Executive Order 12044 also furthered this category of documents.

Federal Register / Vol. 44, No. 144 / Wednesday, July 25, 1979 / Proposed Rules 43477

DEPARTMENT OF AGRICULTURE

Office of the Secretary

[7 CFR Subtitle A]

Title IV, Agricultural Credit Act of 1978; Regulations To Govern Emergency Conservation Programs

AGENCY: Department of Agriculture.

ACTION: Advance Notice of Proposed Rulemaking and Request for Public Comment.

SUMMARY: The Department of Agriculture gives advance notice of forthcoming decisions leading to the implementation of Title IV of the Agricultural Credit Act of 1978, Pub. L. 95–334.

DATE: Comments and suggestions should be submitted on or before August 8, 1979.

ADDRESS: Comments and suggestions should be addressed to Mr. Arnold Miller, Office of the Secretary, Department of Agriculture, Room 117–A, Washington, D.C. 20250, (202) 447–3465.

FOR FURTHER INFORMATION CONTACT: Mrs. Oneida Darley, Assistant to the Deputy Secretary, Room 200–A, Administration Building, U.S. Department of Agriculture, Washington, D.C. 20250, (202) 447–6158.

SUPPLEMENTARY INFORMATION: Title IV of the Agricultural Credit Act of 1978 authorizes certain emergency conservation programs to control wind erosion, rehabilitate agricultural lands, conserve and enhance water supplies and to reduce hazards to life and property in the event of natural disasters. Forthcoming decisions will include those related to developing regulations to govern the programs authorized by Title IV.

The Secretary has directed that implementation of the programs authorized by Title IV be carried out with a view toward ensuring that they are efficiently administered, uniformly responsive in emergencies, and limited to practices and measures that are environmentally and economically supportable. In order to achieve these goals, public comment is requested on such issues as: (1) The criteria to be applied in determining whether assistance under the Act will be provided; (2) whether there should be any fixed monetary limitations on the program assistance, and if so, the amount thereof; and (3) the kinds of measures or practices for which assistance will be provided.

Full implementation of the Title IV programs is conditioned upon the appropriation of funds to carry out those authorities.

Section 401 authorizes a program similar to the emergency conservation measures program currently administered by the Agricultural Stabilization and Conservation Service (ASCS). Section 402 authorizes a program similar to the drought and flood conservation program administered by ASCS in 1977. Section 403 authorizes a program similar to the emergency watershed protection program (Section 216) currently administered by the Soil Conservation Service.

Comments and suggestions made in response to this notice should be received by August 8, 1979, in order to be sure of receiving consideration in connection with development of the proposed rules.

Dated: July 20, 1979.

Jim Williams,

Deputy Secretary.

[FR Doc. 79–23015 Filed 7–24–79; 8:45 am]

BILLING CODE 3410–05–M

Federal Register Finding Aids

Each *Federal Register* contains a number of OFR-prepared research tools, generally termed "finding aids". They appear at the beginning and the end of the issue and will be described, with samples, in the order in which they appear. Included are:

Highlights
Contents
Meetings Announced in This Issue
CFR Parts Affected in This Issue
Reader Aids (at the end of the issue)
    Information and Assistance
    Federal Register Pages and Dates
    CFR Parts Affected During (current month)
    Agency Publication on Assigned Days of the Week
    Table of Effective Dates and Time Periods (first issue of each month)
    CFR Checklist (first issue of each month)
    Agency Abbreviations (first issue of each month)
    Reminders

There are two extremely important finding aids to the Federal Register System which are published separately, the *Federal Register Index* and the *List of CFR Sections Affected (LSA)*. They are described following the finding aids contained in the *FR*, beginning on page 114 of this guide.

Highlights

Highlights. Beginning on the front cover of each day's *FR* and continuing on the next page are the Highlights, a selective listing of the documents in the issue that have wide public interest.

Each Highlights entry includes the page number where the document begins and a brief subject heading, followed by the issuing agency's name and a description of the document. In addition, if the document is a rule, the effective date is given; if it is a proposed rule, the deadline for comments is given.

8-1-79
Vol. 44   No. 149
Pages 45115–45358

federal register

Wednesday
August 1, 1979

Highlights

45123   **Community Funds**   SBA expands sources and amounts which may be injected into local development companies; effective 6–1–79

45116   **Mobile Homes**   FHLBB liberalizes its regulations in order to make loans more available and affordable; effective 8–31–79

45247   **National Fire Codes**   GSA/OFR request proposals from the public to assist in amending existing safety standards

45246   **National Fire Codes**   GSA/OFR request comments on techincal report; comments by 10–5–79

45298   **Unlawful Trade Practices**   Treasury/ATF proposes rules prohibited by the Federal Alcohol Administration; comments by 10–30–79 (Part III of this issue)

45141   **Truth in Lending**   FRS proposes a rule on calculation and disclosure of annual percentage rates; comments by 10–15–79

45240   **Data Collection**   EPA identifies certain activities to be undertaken during the next six-month period for specific industrial point source categories

45120   **Licenses**   SBA adopts rules on small business investment companies; effective 8–1–79

CONTINUED INSIDE

Note the listings for Sunshine Act Meetings and Separate Parts of This Issue at the end of the Highlights.

II   Federal Register / Vol. 44, No. 149 / Wednesday, August 1, 1979 / Highlights

Highlights

FEDERAL REGISTER Published daily, Monday through Friday, (not published on Saturdays, Sundays, or on official holidays), by the Office of the Federal Register, National Archives and Records Service, General Services Administration, Washington, D.C. 20408, under the Federal Register Act (49 Stat. 500, as amended; 44 U.S.C. Ch. 15) and the regulations of the Administrative Committee of the Federal Register (1 CFR Ch. I). Distribution is made only by the Superintendent of Documents, U.S. Government Printing Office, Washington, D.C. 20402.

The **Federal Register** provides a uniform system for making available to the public regulations and legal notices issued by Federal agencies. These include Presidential proclamations and Executive Orders and Federal agency documents having general applicability and legal effect, documents required to be published by Act of Congress and other Federal agency documents of public interest. Documents are on file for public inspection in the Office of the Federal Register the day before they are published, unless earlier filing is requested by the issuing agency.

The **Federal Register** will be furnished by mail to subscribers, free of postage, for $5.00 per month or $50 per year, payable in advance. The charge for individual copies of 75 cents for each issue, or 75 cents for each group of pages as actually bound. Remit check or money order, made payable to the Superintendent of Documents, U.S. Government Printing Office, Washington, D.C. 20402.

There are no restrictions on the republication of material appearing in the **Federal Register**.

Area Code 202-523-5240

Contents

Contents. Following the Highlights is the Contents, a comprehensive alphabetical listing by agency name of *all* documents in the issue. Under each agency name the documents are arranged by type—Rules, Proposed Rules, or Notices—and each entry includes the page number where the document begins and a brief description of what it is about. (Sunshine Act meetings are included under the Notices listing).

Presidential Documents are listed at the beginning of the Contents under the heading "The President," just as they appear first in the issue.

The indentation-style format will be repeated in a separate monthly publication based on this table of contents, the *Federal Register Index.*

Note the cross references from major departments to subordinate sub-agencies.

Meetings Announced in This Issue

Meetings Announced in This Issue. At the end of the Contents is a special section listing meetings announced within the issue, a real help to the reader watching for one particular meeting announcement. This also is arranged by agency name and includes the date on which each meeting is scheduled to be held, as well as the group meeting.

III

Contents

Federal Register

Vol. 44, No. 149

Wednesday, August 1, 1979

CFR Parts Affected
in This Issue

CFR Parts Affected in This Issue. The final finding aid appearing in the preliminary pages of each day's *FR* is a list of CFR Parts Affected in This Issue. Under each *CFR* title the rules and proposed rules published in the issue are listed, arranged by part number, along with the page numbers where the relevant documents begin. Examples of the way in which CFR parts are affected include additions, amendments, deletions, and revocations.

The Reader Aids section at the end of each issue includes an expansion on this table, a cumulative list of the parts affected so far during the current month.

VIII   Federal Register / Vol. 44, No. 149 / Wednesday, August 1, 1979 / Contents

CFR PARTS AFFECTED IN THIS ISSUE

A cumulative list of the parts affected this month can be found in the Reader Aids section at the end of this issue.

7 CFR
53.......................................45320
1464..................................45115
1806..................................45115

10 CFR
212.....................................45352
Proposed Rules:
903.....................................45141

12 CFR
201.....................................45115
545.....................................45116
Proposed Rules:
226.....................................45141
509.....................................45175
509a...................................45175
550.....................................45175
566.....................................45175

13 CFR
107.....................................45120
108.....................................45123

16 CFR
Proposed Rules:
Ch. I...................................45178
13.......................................45181

17 CFR
Proposed Rules:
1...45192

19 CFR
Proposed Rules:
Ch. I...................................45333

24 CFR
Proposed Rules:
Subtitle A...........................45342
Subtitle B...........................45342

26 CFR
Proposed Rules:
1...45192
601.....................................45192

27 CFR
Proposed Rules:
Ch. I...................................45326
6...45298
8...45298
10.......................................45298
11.......................................45298

81.......................................45210
162.....................................45218

43 CFR
Public Land Orders:
5675....................................45133
5676....................................45133

44 CFR
64.......................................45133
65 (2 documents)...........45136, 45137
Proposed Rules:
67 (6 documents)..........45225–45227

45 CFR
302.....................................45137

47 CFR
Proposed Rules:
15.......................................45227

50 CFR
32.......................................45137
Proposed Rules:
652.....................................45227

Reader Aids

Reader Aids. At the end of each day's issue is the Reader Aids Section, which is designed to help the reader find specific information in the Federal Register System, as distinguished from the finding aids in the preliminary pages which are more oriented toward one particular issue.

Information and Assistance. Always first at the back of the book is the listing of OFR telephone numbers to call for specific areas of inquiry.

Federal Register Pages and Dates. This is a parallel table of the inclusive pages and corresponding dates for the current month's *FR.*

CFR Parts Affected During (current month). This is a cumulative list of *CFR* parts affected by rules and proposed rules appearing so far each month in the *FR,* in this case for the first 10 days of August. (Note the date at the top of the page.)

i

Reader Aids

See below page 118 for telephone information and assistance.

Federal Register

Vol. 44, No. 156

Friday, August 10, 1979

INFORMATION AND ASSISTANCE

Questions and requests for specific information may be directed to the following numbers. General inquiries may be made by dialing 202-523-5240.

Federal Register, Daily Issue:

202-783-3238	Subscription orders (GPO)
202-275-3054	Subscription problems (GPO)
	"Dial-a-Reg" (recorded summary of highlighted documents appearing in next day's issue):
202-523-5022	Washington, D.C.
312-663-0884	Chicago, Ill.
˙˃ -688-6694	Los Angeles, Calif.
	Scheduling of documents for publi ⸝s, U.S. ⸝⸝ies of documents app⸝
275-3030	⸝⸝⸝

Other Publications and Servi⸝⸝

523-5239	TTY for the Deaf
523-5230	U.S. Government Manual
523-3408	Automation
523-4534	Special Projects
523-3517	Privacy Act Compilation

FEDERAL REGISTER PAGES AND DATES, AUGUST

45115–45358	1
45359–45586	2
45587–45916	3
45917–46248	6
46249–46426	7
46427–46776	8
46777–47028	9
47029–47262	10

CFR PARTS AFFECTED DURING AUGUST

At the end of each month, the Office of the Federal Register publishes separately a list of CFR Sections Affected (LSA), which lists parts and sections affected by documents published since the revision date of each title.

5 CFR

Ch. XIV	45359
210	45587
430	45587
432	45591
⸝⸝	47029
	47029
⸝	462⸝
925	
926	
947	⸝0
979	⸝17
993	⸝6250
1011	46777
1435	45596
1464	45115
1806	45115
1822	46250
1861	46250
1863	46250
1872	46250
1945	46250
1951	46250
1955	46250
2852	45602

Proposed Rules:

Ch. XVIII	46852
⸝⸝	4646⸝

82	46263
97	45605
201	45359
309	45605
318	45606
381	45606

⸝roposed Rules:

	45912
3⸝⸝	45912
376	45912
391	⸝5631
420	
485	45⸝⸝
503	46854
505	46854
903	45141

12 CFR

4	46263
7	46428
201	45115
205	46432
217	46434, 46436, 46437
226	46438
329	46264
⸝⸝	45375
	46440, 46441
	46445
	⸝⸝444

Agency Publication on Assigned Days of the Week. Certain agencies have agreed to publish their documents on assigned days of the week on a two day schedule (either Monday/Thursday or Tuesday/Friday). This reduces the number of issues a reader must look at if interested in one particular agency's publication.

[Published only in the first issue of each month]

Table of Effective Dates and Time Periods. This is a table for use in computing advance notice requirements and public response time limits for *FR* documents published during the current month.

[Published only in the first issue of each month]

ii   **Federal Register** / Vol. 44, No. 149 / Wednesday, August 1, 1979 / Reader Aids

AGENCY PUBLICATION ON ASSIGNED DAYS OF THE WEEK

The following agencies have agreed to publish all documents on two assigned days of the week (Monday/Thursday or Tuesday/Friday).

This is a voluntary program. (See OFR NOTICE FR 32914, August 6, 1976.)

Monday	Tuesday	Wednesday	Thursday	Friday
DOT/SECRETARY*	USDA/ASCS		DOT/SECRETARY*	USDA/ASCS
DOT/COAST GUARD	USDA/APHIS		DOT/COAST GUARD	USDA/APHIS
DOT/FAA	USDA/FNS		DOT/FAA	USDA/FNS
DOT/FHWA	USDA/FSQS		DOT/FHWA	USDA/FSQS
DOT/FRA	USDA/REA		DOT/FRA	USDA/REA
DOT/NHTSA	MSPB/OPM		DOT/NHTSA	MSPB/OPM
DOT/RSPA	LABOR		DOT/RSPA	LABOR
DOT/SLS	HEW/FDA		DOT/SLS	HEW/FDA
DOT/UMTA			DOT/UMTA	
CSA			CSA	

Documents normally scheduled for publication on a day that will be a Federal holiday will be published the next work day following the holiday.

Comments on this program are still invited. Comments should be submitted to the Day-of-the-Week Program Coordinator. Office of the Federal Register, National Archives and Records Service, General Services Administration, Washington, D.C. 20408

*NOTE: As of July 2, 1979, all agencies in the Department of Transportation, will publish on the Monday/Thursday schedule.

TABLE OF EFFECTIVE DATES AND TIME PERIODS—AUGUST 1979

This table is for use in computing dates certain in connection with documents which are published in the Federal Register subject to advance notice requirements or which impose time limits on public response.

Federal Agencies using this table in calculating time requirements for submissions must allow sufficient extra time for Federal Register scheduling procedures.

In computing dates certain, the day after publication counts as one. All succeeding days are counted except that when a date certain falls on a weekend or holiday, it is moved forward to the next Federal business day. (See 1 CFR 18.17)

A new table will be published in the first issue of each month.

Dates of FR publication	15 days after publication	30 days after publication	45 days after publication	60 days after publication	90 days after publication
August 1	August 16	August 31	September 17	October 1	October 30
August 2	August 17	September 4	September 17	October 1	October 31
August 3	August 20	September 4	September 17	October 2	November 1
August 6	August 21	September 5	September 20	October 5	November 5
August 7	August 22	September 6	September 21	October 9	November 5
August 8	August 23	September 7	September 24	October 9	November 6
August 9	August 24	September 10	September 24	October 9	November 7
August 10	August 27	September 10	September 24	October 9	November 8
August 13	August 28	September 12	~mber 27	October 12	Novem~
~4	August 29	Septem~	~8	October 15	
	August 30	~		October 15	
	~t 31			~ober ~~	

CFR Checklist. The checklist is a list of the revision dates and prices of current *CFR* volumes.

[Published only in the first issue of each month]

CFR CHECKLIST; 1978/1979 ISSUANCES

This checklist, prepared by the Office of the Federal Register, is published in the first issue of each month. It is arranged in the order of CFR titles, and shows the revision date and price of the volumes of the Code of Federal Regulations issued to date for 1978/1979. New units issued during the month are announced on the back cover of the daily **Federal Register** as they become available.

For a checklist of current CFR volumes comprising a complete CFR set, see the latest issue of the LSA (List of CFR Sections Affected), which is revised monthly.

The annual rate for subscription service to all revised volumes is $450 domestic, $115 additional for foreign mailing.

Order from Superintendent of Documents, Government Printing Office, Washington, D.C. 20402.

CFR Unit (Rev. as of Jan. 1, 1979):

Title	Price
1	$3.00
2 [Reserved]	
4	4.50

7 Parts:

0–52	6.75
?–209	5.00
?99	6 ?

24 Parts:

0–499	8.00
25	7.00

26 Parts:

1 (§§ 1.301–1.400)	5.50
1 (§§ 1.501–1.640)	6.00
1 (§§ 1.641–1.850)	6.50
300–499	6.00
600–end	1.25

 ̄ Unit (Rev. as of

Chapter 18, Parts:

1–52 (Vol. I, Rev. 7/31/78)	5.25
1–52 (Vol. II, Rev. 7/31/78)	7.00
1–52 (Vol. III, Rev. 7/31/78)	5.75

Chapters:

19–100	4.50
CFR Index	5.00
101–end	8.50

CFR Unit (Rev. as of Oct. 1, 1978):

42 Parts:

1–399	6.00
400–end	5.50

43 Parts:

1–999	4.25
1000–end	6.50

44 [Reserved]

45 Parts:

1–99	4.75
100–149	5.75
150- 199	5.25
	3.50
	8.25

Agency Abbreviations. The Highlights and Reminders sections use abbreviations from this list.

[Published only in the first issue of each month]

AGENCY ABBREVIATIONS
Used in Highlights and Reminders

(This List Will Be Published Monthly in First Issue of Month.)

USDA Agriculture Department
AMS Agricultural Marketing Service
APHIS Animal and Plant Health Inspection Service
ASCS Agricultural Stabilization and Conservation Service
CCC Commodity Credit Corporation
CEA Commodity Exchange Authority
EMS Export Marketing Service
EOA Energy Office, Department of Agriculture
ESCS Economics, Statistics, and Cooperatives Serv?
FmHA Farmers Home Administration
FAS Foreign Agricultural Service
?deral Crop Insurance Corr?
?on Ser?

FERC Federal Energy Regulatory Commission
OHADOE Hearings and Appeals Office, Energy Department
SEPA Southeastern Power Administration
SWPA Southwestern Power Administration
WAPA Western Area Power Administration

HEW Health, Education, and Welfare Department
ADAMHA Alcohol, Drug Abuse, and Mental Health Administration
CDC Center for Disease Control
ESNC Educational Statistics National Center
FDA Food and Drug Administration
HCFA Health Care Financing Administration
HDSO Human Development Services Office
HRA Health Resources Administration
? Health Services Administration
?seum Services Institute
?al Institutes of Hea?
?l Insti?

Reminders

Reminders. Each day's issue ends with a list of reminders, usually two categories—Rules Going Into Effect Today and the List of Public Laws recently signed by the President. In addition, each *Wednesday* the section is expanded to include the following categories: Next Week's Deadlines for Comments on Proposed Rules, Next Week's Meetings, Next Week's Public Hearings, and Documents Relating to Federal Grant Programs (which includes Rules Going Into Effect, Deadlines for Comments on Proposed Rules, Applications Deadlines, Meetings, and Other Items of Interest).

vi   Federal Register / Vol. 44, No. 149 / Wednesday, August 1, 1979 / Reader Aids

REMINDERS

The items in this list were editorially compiled as an aid to Federal Register users. Inclusion or exclusion from this list has no legal significance. Since this list is intended as a reminder, it does not include effective dates that occur within 14 days of publication.

Rules Going Into Effect Today

AGRICULTURE DEPARTMENT

Agriculture Marketing Service—

40491   7–11–79 / Cotton and cottonseed; revision in fees

COMMERCE DEPARTMENT

Census Bureau—

38832   7–3–79 / Requirement for employer identification number and change in value requirement for filing of shipper's export declaration

[Corrected at 44 FR 40064, 7–9–79]

COMMODITY FUTURES TRADING COMMISSION

25431   5–1–79 / Reports by futures commission merchants and foreign brokers; carrying and reporting the total open long and short positions in omnibus accounts

★ ★ ★ ★ ★ ★ ★

Next Week's Deadlines for Comments On Proposed Rules

AGRICULTURE DEPARTMENT

Agricultural Marketing Service—

43286   7–24–79 / Handling of fresh prunes grown in designated counties in Washington and in Umatilla County, Oreg.; comments by 8–8–79

32706   6–7–79 / Navel oranges grown in Arizona and part of California; establishment of separate district, comments by 8–6–79

Animal and Plant Health Inspection Service—

★ ★ ★ ★ ★ ★ ★

Next Week's Meetings

AGING, FEDERAL COUNCIL

40725   7–12–79 / Long Term Care Committee, Washington, D.C. (open), 8–6–79

ARTS AND HUMANITIES, NATIONAL FOUNDATION

42343   7–19–79 / Humanities Panel Advisory Committee, Washington, D.C. (closed), 8–6 through 8–10–79

CIVIL RIGHTS COMMISSION

43031   7–23–79 / California Advisory Committee; Los Angeles. Calif. (open), 8–10–79

Next Week's Public Hearings

AGRICULTURE DEPARTMENT

Forest Service—

42300   7–19–79 / Tuolumne wild and scenic river study report and environmental impact statement, Modesto, Calif., 8–7–79

42300   7–19–79 / Tuolumne wild and scenic river study report and environmental impact statement, San Francisco, Calif., 8–9–79

42300   7–19–79 / Tuolumne wild and scenic river study report and environmental impact statement, Oakland, Calif., 8–11–79

Transportation Office—

40368   7–10–79 / Rural Transportation Advisory Task Force, Mitchell, S.Dak., 8–8–79

ENERGY DEPARTMENT

42094   7–18–79 / Urban wastes demonstration facilities guarantee program, New Orleans, La., 8–9–79

Economic Regulatory Administration—

42545   7–19–79 / Motor gasoline allocation level provisions; amendments, Chicago, Ill., 8–9–79

40325   7–10–79 / Propane increased non-product costs; Washington, D.C., 8–8–79

Western Area Power Administration—

42767   7–20–79 / Central Valley Project; proposed rate order, Sacramento, Calif., 8–7–79

FOREIGN LANGUAGE AND INTERNATIONAL STUDIES, PRESIDENT'S COMMISSION

43808   7–26–79 / Federal Advisory Committee, Honolulu, Hawaii, 8–9 and 8–10–79

List of Public Laws

Note: No public bills which have become law were received by the Office of the Federal Register for inclusion in today's **List of Public Laws.**

Last Listing July 30, 1979

Documents Relating to Federal Grant Programs

This is a list of documents relating to Federal grant programs which were published in the **Federal Register** during the previous week.

DEADLINES FOR COMMENTS ON PROPOSED RULES

43712   7–26–79 / Commerce/EDA—Supplementary grant rates for public works project; comments by 9–24–79

44096   7–26–79 / HEW/OE—Family contribution schedules; Basic Opportunity Educational Grant; comments by 9–10–79

APPLICATIONS DEADLINES

43330   7–24–79 / Commerce/MBEO—Financial assistance application announcement; apply by 8–17–79

Federal Register Index

The *Federal Register Index* is a separate publication. It is based on a consolidation of the entries appearing in the Contents of each day's *FR*. The entries are found primarily under the names of the issuing agencies along with broad subject headings.

The *Index* is published monthly on a cumulative basis; thus the December Index is also the Annual Index (consolidating January through December).

The *Index* also includes a list of Privacy Act publications, a Table of Federal Register Pages and Dates (see page 115 of this guide), and, on a quarterly basis, a Guide to Freedom of Information Indexes.

The *Federal Register Index* comes as part of the *FR* subscription, or can be purchased separately.

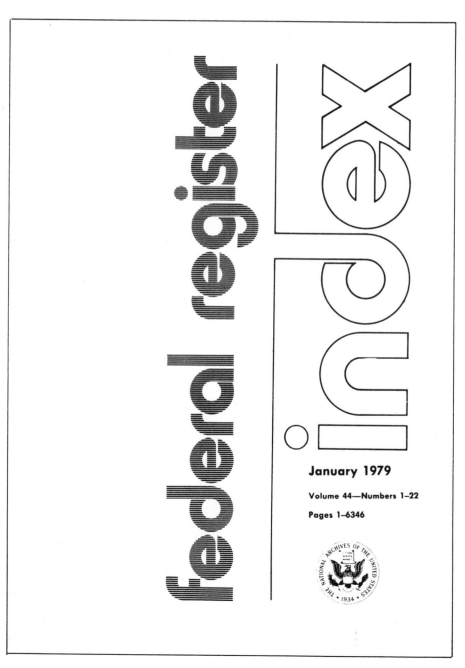

January 1979

Volume 44—Numbers 1–22

Pages 1–6346

FEDERAL REGISTER INDEX, January 1979

THE PRESIDENT

(See also Executive Office of President)

EXECUTIVE ORDERS

Administration, Office of; seal (EO 12112), 1073

Civil Service Commission and labor-management in the Federal service (EO 12107), 1055

Eı ,loyee Retirement Income Security Act, transfer of functions (EO 12108), 1065

Environmental effects abroad of Federal actions (EO 12114), 1957

Equal employment enforcement functions, transfer (EO 12106), 1053

Executive schedule, placement of certain positions in levels IV and V (EO 12111), 1071

Federal advisory committees; continuance of certain (EO 12110), 1069

Federal physicians comparability allowance (EO 12109), 1067

Food stamps, issuance by Postal Service (EO 12116), 4647

Independent water project review (EO 12113), 1955

Panama, permanent American cemetery (EO 12115), 4645

MEMORANDUMS

International trade agreements (January 4), 1933

Taiwan, United States relations with the people on (December 30), 1075

DESIGNATIONS

National security information, classification by Director of White House Military Office (January 26), 5639

PROCLAMATIONS

Bolts, nuts and screw imports; duty increase (Proc. 4632), 1697

Color television receivers and subassemblies, orderly marketing agreements and limitation on imports (Proc. 4634), 5633

Special observances:
Heart Month, American (Proc. 4633), 2563

Sugar and sirups, import fees; imposition (Proc. 4631), 1

EXECUTIVE AGENCIES

ACCIDENTS

See National Transportation Safety Board.

ACTION

NOTICES

Competitive National VISTA grants, proposed procedures, 2634

Foster Grandparent and Senior Companion Programs; income eligibility levels, 1768

Improving Government regulations:
Regulatory agenda; semiannual, 1996

Regulatory agenda; semiannual, 1996

Special Volunteer Programs; competitive demonstration grants; availability of funds, 5919

ACTUARIES, JOINT BOARD FOR ENROLLMENT

NOTICES

Annuitants, limits on compensation; withdrawn, 3342

Authority delegations:
Africa Bureau Field Posts, Mission Director et al.; loan and grant agreements, 2446

Bangladesh, Mission Director; contracting functions, 2050

Contracting officer Arthur Bjorlykke; execution of contracts, grants, etc., 2049

Fiji, Regional Development Officer;

PRIVACY ACT PUBLICATIONS

ACTUARIES, JOINT BOARD FOR ENROLLMENT

NOTICES

Systems of records; annual publication, 5212

AGRICULTURE DEPARTMENT

NOTICES

Systems of records., 5171

ARMY DEPARTMENT

RULES

Implementation, 5651

CENTRAL INTELLIGENCE AGENCY

NOTICES

Systems of records, 4518

COMMERCE DEPARTMENT

NOTICES

Systems of records, 3308

DEFENSE LOGISTICS AGENCY

NOTICES

Systems of records, 5700

DEFENSE MAPPING AGENCY

NOTICES

Systems of records, 4882

EDUCATION OFFICE

NOTICES

Systems of records, 957

FEDERAL COMMUNICATIONS COMMISSION

NOTICES

Systems of records, 1457

FEDERAL MARITIME COMMISSION

NOTICES

Systems of records, 5941

FOREIGN CLAIMS SETTLEMENT COMMISSION

NOTICES

Systems of records; annual publication, 5714

HOUSING AND URBAN DEVELOPMENT DEPARTMENT

NOTICES

Systems of records, 2430, 5207

INTERNATIONAL COMMUNICATION AGENCY

NOTICES

Systems of records, 4856

JUSTICE DEPARTMENT

NOTICES

Systems of records, 4542

FEDERAL REGISTER PAGES AND DATES

Pages	Date	Pages	Date
1–748	Jan. 2	2563–3019	12
749–1070	3	3021–3252	15
1071–1355	4	3253–3449	16
1357–1696	5	3451–3668	17
1697–1954	8	3669–3942	18
1955–2163	9	3943–4430	19
2165–2351	10	4431–4644	22
2353–2562	11	4645–4931	23

List of CFR Sections
Affected (LSA)

The *List of CFR Sections Affected* (*LSA*) is designed to lead users of the *CFR* to amendatory actions published in the *FR*. Entries are by *CFR* title, chapter, part, and section, and indicate the nature of the change (i.e. additions or deletions). Proposed rules are listed at the end of appropriate titles except for Title 41, in which proposed rules follow each chapter.

The *LSA* is issued monthly in cumulative form, keyed to the annual revision schedule of the *CFR* volume(s) represented. If a particular *LSA* is an annual cumulation, it is so noted on the cover.

In addition to the basic listing each *LSA* contains a complete explanation on the inside cover (especially helpful is the "How to Use" paragraph). Also included are a Checklist of Current CFR Volumes (giving each volume's price and most recent revision date), a Parallel Table of Authorities and Rules, and a Table of Federal Register Issue Pages and Dates (*see* page 117 of this guide).

The *LSA* comes as part of the *FR* subscription or may be purchased separately.

List of CFR Sections Affected

December 1979

SAVE THIS ISSUE
  for Annual Cumulation
  of Titles 1–16*

CONTAINING:

  TITLES 1–16
    *Changes Jan. 2, 1979
    through Dec. 31, 1979

  TITLES 17–27
    Changes April 2, 1979
    through Dec. 31, 1979

  TITLES 28–41
    Changes July 2, 1979
    ⸱gh Dec. 31, 1979

LSA—LIST OF CFR SECTIONS AFFECTED

The LIST OF CFR SECTIONS AFFECTED is designed to lead users of the Code of Federal Regulations (CFR) to amendatory actions published in the Federal Register (FR). It should be shelved with current CFR volumes. Entries are by CFR title, chapter, part, and section. Proposed rules are listed at the end of appropriate titles, except for Title 41, in which proposed rules follow each chapter.

HOW TO USE THIS FINDING AID

The CFR is revised annually according to the following schedule:

Titles 1–16—as of Jan. 1
17–27—as of April 1
28–41—as of July 1
42–50—as of Oct. 1

To bring these regulations up to date, consult this LIST OF CFR SECTIONS AFFECTED for any changes, additions, or deletions published after the revision date of the volume you are using. Then check the CUMULATIVE LIST OF PARTS AFFECTED appearing at the front of the latest Federal Register for less detailed but

Ci
Exan

ISSU

Th
ANN
1–16
ANN
ANN

PAR
A
cited

TABI
A
num

INDE
Ar
annu
to th

INQ
Th
assis
phor

SU
come
Arch

CHECKLIST OF CURRENT CFR VOLUMES   3

(Comprising a complete CFR set)

Title	Price	Revision Date
1, 2 (2 Reserved)	$3.00	Jan. 1, 1979
3 (Compilation of 1978 Presidential documents and Parts 100 and 101)	6.00	Jan. 1, 1979
4	5.50	Jan. 1, 1979
5	7.50	Jul. 1, 1979
6	3.00	July 1, 1979
7 (Parts 0–52)	6.75	Jan. 1, 1979
(Parts 53–209)	5.00	Jan. 1, 1979
(Parts 210–699)	11.00	Jan. 1, 1979
(Parts 700–899)	6.00	Jan. 1, 1979
(Parts 900–944)	5.25	Jan. 1, 1979
(Parts 945–980)	3.75	Jan. 1, 1979
(Parts 981–999)	3.75	Jan. 1, 1979

(Parts
(Parts
(Parts
(Parts
(Parts
(Parts
(Part

156   PARALLEL TABLE OF AUTHORITIES AND RULES

Additions to Table 1, July through December 1979

This table lists the sections of the U.S. Code and U.S. Statutes at Large and Presidential documents which are being added to Table 1 as a result of authority citations carried in the *Federal Register* from July through December 1979. Recent legislation is carried by public law number.

Table 1 is in the CFR Index and finding aids revised as of July 1, 1979.

In order to determine the *Federal Register* page numbers of the parallel CFR citations, consult the List of CFR Sections Affected above.

U.S. Code:	CFR	5 U.S.C.:	CFR
2 U.S.C.:		5335	5 Part 930
431	11 Parts 100, 110, 114	5372	5 Part 930
441b	11 Parts 100, 110, 114	5385	5 Part 534

8
9
10 (Part
(Part
11
12 (Part
(Part
13
14 (Part
(Part
(Part
15
16 (Parts
(Parts
(Part
17
18 (Parts
(Part
19
20 (Parts
(Parts
(Part
21 (Parts
(Parts
(Parts
(Parts
(Parts
(Part

5 U.S.
552

49
552a

552b
553

10   LSA—LIST OF CFR SECTIONS AFFECTED

CHANGES JANUARY 2 THROUGH DECEMBER 31, 1979

Title 4, Chapter I—Continued   Page

91.4 (b) revised _____ 18639
92.3 (b), (c), (d) revised _____ 18639

Chapter II—Federal Claims Collection Standards (General Accounting Office—Department of Justice)

101.1 Revised _____ 22701
102.2 Revised _____ 22702
102.4 Redesignated as 102.5; new

TITLE 5—ADMINISTRATIVE PERSONNEL

Chapter I—Office of Personnel Management   Page

Chapter heading revised _____ 3943
Chapter I Special transitional regulation No. 1 _____ 3440
Chapter I nomenclature changes_ 47523, 76747

Telephone Information and Assistance

Questions and requests for specific information may be directed to the following numbers. General inquiries may be made by dialing 202–523–5240.

FEDERAL REGISTER, Daily Issue:
 Subscription orders (GPO) 202–783–3238
 Subscription problems (GPO) 783–3238
 "Dial-a-Regulation" (recorded summary of highlighted documents appearing in next day's issue):
  Washington, D.C 202–523–5022
  Chicago, Ill 312–663–0884
  Los Angeles, Calif 213–688–6694
 Scheduling of documents for publication 202–523–3187
 Photocopies of documents appearing in the *Federal Register* 523–5240
 Corrections 523–5237
 Public Inspection Desk 523–5215
 Finding Aids 523–5227
PUBLIC BRIEFINGS: "How to Use the *Federal Register*" 523–5235
CODE OF FEDERAL REGULATIONS (CFR) 523–3419
 Finding Aids 523–5227
PRESIDENTIAL PAPERS:
 Executive Orders and Proclamations 523–5233
 Weekly Compilation of Presidential Documents 523–5235
 Public Papers of the Presidents 523–5235
 Index 523–5235
PUBLIC LAWS:
 Public Law dates and numbers 523–5266 (5282)
 Slip Laws 523–5266 (5282)
  Slip Law orders (GPO) 275–3030
UNITED STATES GOVERNMENT MANUAL 523–5230
AUTOMATION 523–3408
SPECIAL PROJECTS 523–4534
PRIVACY ACT INFORMATION 523–3517
LIBRARY 523–5240
TTY FOR THE DEAF 523–5239